WEED 'EM AND REAP
A Weed Eater Reader

WEED 'EM AND REAP

A Weed Eater Reader

Roger Welsch

FALCONGUIDE®

GUILFORD, CONNECTICUT
HELENA, MONTANA

AN IMPRINT OF THE GLOBE PEQUOT PRESS

Cover design by Jane Sheppard
Front cover photo by Photos.com
All photos of Roger Welsch by Lisa Linnemeyer, New Perspective Photography
Text design by Nancy Freeborn

Library of Congress Cataloging-in-Publication Data

Welsch, Roger L.
    Weed 'em and reap : a weed eater reader / Roger Welsch.
        p. cm.
    Includes bibliographical references and index.
    ISBN 0-7627-3907-X
 1. Cookery (Wild foods)—Humor. 2. Wild plants, Edible—Humor. I. Title.
    TX823.W4475 2006
    641.5'63.dc22   2005015625

Manufactured in the United States of America
First Edition/First Printing

 Text printed on recycled paper.

To buy books in quantity for corporate use
or incentives, call **(800) 962–0973, ext. 4551,**
or e-mail **premiums@GlobePequot.com.**

A weed is but
an unloved flower.

—Ella Wheeler Wilcox, "The Weed"

Contents

Acknowledgments

For generously sharing their plant wisdom with me, I am especially indebted to my tribal friends and relatives, to Kay Young, and to Dick Gray. Special thanks, too, to Linda and my children, who for years have faced hot and cold unidentifieds and unidentifiables on their dinner plates— or straight off bushes, or out of the ground. And my eternal gratitude to all those intrepid souls who over the millennia had the courage to try various parts of various plants, especially those whose luck ran out when an experimental nibble went bad.

An Introduction and Some Fair Warnings

There are lots of books out there about how to accurately and skillfully identify and cook wild foods, but not very many about first-rate, industrial-grade weed eating. I'm not a botanist or chef, but I am an accomplished and widely acclaimed eater. I am, in fact, a walking billboard for my gustatory endeavors. And I am goofily enthusiastic about free food, fun food, and even defiant food. I love the idea of eating stuff that no one else eats and of spending days in the woods, prairies, and wetlands watching the wonders of nature. I like good tastes. I also very much admire the notion of being out on a camping trip and amazing everyone else around the campfire by serving up a salad, stew, vegetable, tea, or dessert that comes as a total surprise—and is made out of something found within yelling distance of our tents.

That's what this book is about—things like that. And those things can be found anywhere in America, probably anywhere in the world. See, every area has a different set of plants, so I can't really tell you what you're going to find in your part of the world. I know how I like my weeds cooked, but I have no way of knowing what you like. I can't eat shellfish—and heaven only knows what *you* can't eat. I'm no good at all at drawing illustrations and not much better with a camera. I love to write, but I don't do well at writing long, detailed descriptions of how a plant's archimemes join up with its lancelots to form the unique dipowad exclusive to the mangible genre of glucogyrenes.

Besides, as I started off above, there are plenty of books like that, specifically written for your region and for your tastes by experts. My intent in the following pages is to tell you some stories about eating weeds. I'm good at story-telling, they tell me, so that's what I do. My hope is not to make a biologist or gourmet cook out of you but to convince you that it really is fun knowing something about wild plants and eating them. You won't come off the last page an expert in anything at all, but hopefully you will close the book with a new eagerness to know more about plants and cooking them and a new enthusiasm for wandering around the wilds. And for eating good stuff. And for picking up more specific and specialized books about your precise interests and region.

The very best book I know of for my interests and my immediate geography is *Wild Seasons: Gathering and Cooking Wild Plants of the Great Plains* (University of Nebraska Press, 1993), which happens to be written by a dear friend of mine, Kay Young. I wish there were a book like hers for every state in the Union. I highly recommend Kay's book, of course, but in all honesty it won't do you a lot of good in Florida or Alaska. It's about America's central Plains. I can't even rec-ommend a book for you because who knows where "you" are? Hopefully, you know where you are, and you know where the library or a good bookstore is, and you can go there and do some scouting around before you go traipsing around in the wild, eat some death camas, and poison yourself.

And that's what you should do (scouting around, not poisoning yourself). Let this book be something of an inspiration to lead you onto the paths of wilderness munchery! Find an expert for your region—you'll be surprised how many there are—or go to the World Wide Web and seek out information about specific plants. Take classes and workshops. Spend some time with veteran cooks or pioneers, even within your own family. Heck, if there isn't a book about wild plants and cookery specific to your immediate area or state, maybe you'll be the one to write it!

Mostly I want you to be safe, well fed, and excited about the world around you. I want you to share the kind of good times and the kind of good eating I've had with wild foods. Much has been written and said about "soul food"; about food being far more than nutrition, economy, convenience, or even taste. And it is true—food is heavier on meaning than most people know or imagine. So hopefully your experiences with wild foods will bring you not only good health and happy tables but also memories that last well after the taste of the food is gone from your lips.

The Good, The Bad, The Ugly, and the Really, Really, Really Ugly

First, the good news about nutrition and foraging. Nobody wants to get scurvy or rickets or simply suffer from basic malnutrition. You're not going to. Trust me. The forager should strive for dietary balance, obviously. You can't live on mulberries for two years. Most of us, however, are eating wild foods along with all kinds of other stuff. Our systems tell us what we need, and when we have a sudden urge to eat acidic greens, there's some reason to believe our bodies need acidic greens. Still, Americans are so overnutritioned already that more of us are killed by the poisons generated by worrying about nutrition than by bad nutrition itself. You could survive on nothing but mulberries (or beans, or buffalo) for a week and be none the worse for the wear because you would soon be tired of mulberries or out of mulberries and move on to something else edible, abundant, and in season.

On the other hand, if you really are in some sort of serious jam—abandoned in the Canadian woods, stranded on an island in the Boundary Waters, injured and stuck in a Colorado canyon with no clear indication anyone is looking for you or knows where you are—think of nutritional balance strategically. That is, not in terms of days or weeks, but months. Eat what you have, what's available. Make intelligent choices. Don't be a pig. Eat as much variety as you can. Remember that the wild foods you are eating contain many times the vitamin content you would expect from commercially available foods, even fresh foods like lettuce or cabbage. Four little rose hips picked from a wild rosebush down by the river on my farm contain the vitamin C of an orange! If you're scraping out a living on wild greens, roots, berries, and fruits, you're likely to be better off nutritionally than most Americans in urban ghettos or on Indian reservations struggling on commodity foods—or for that matter, probably better than some teenage kid who lives for five years on nothing but fast foods and candy bars.

Let's keep this whole thing on the fun level for the

moment. The information, and more precisely the attitude, you will hopefully gain here will serve you well in dire circumstances. But for me, eating wild is about fun, so let's not take it too seriously—except for what I have to tell you next.

And Now the Bad News: A Serious and Important Caution!

Throughout this book I warn you to be careful when harvesting food in the wild and to be sure, *very* sure, of what the plants are that you are gathering for your table. There are a lot of very dangerous plants in the wild, some fatally poisonous, and it just isn't worth the risk. With very little instruction, research, and training, however, you will be as safe grazing in the wild as you are in a supermarket, and maybe even safer.

However—and this is a really important "however," so pay attention—even safe and edible wild plants these days are sometimes made dangerous by the constant and pernicious efforts of our fellow man, idiot that he is. Most of my life I have been utterly dazzled by the cosmic, industrial-grade ignorance of people who jog for their health on busy highways and streets, wading through clouds of toxic vehicle exhaust, often dressed in dark (even camouflage-pattern!) clothing— at night! It's a peculiar form of suicide. But these fitness nuts will have very healthy-looking corpses, I imagine.

I discourage gathering wild foods along busy highways where exhaust fumes poison the air, automotive effluvia splats and splashes on roadside plants, people throw dirty diapers blithely out the windows of their moving cars, maintenance workers spray God-only-knows-what chemicals to kill God-only-knows-what "weeds" for God-only-knows-what reasons. This danger can even exist in heavily agricultural areas that may seem bucolic enough but are drenched with Agent Orange–like poisons to kill crop pests, both weeds and insects. Plants like cattails or arrowhead obviously carry with them whatever pathogens might be in their host waterways. Gather only from the cleanest water and then clean plants carefully, if possible rinsing your harvest with water purified via water purification tablets, chlorine, or at least boiling. (Do note, however, that some toxins like heavy metals are not affected by boiling.) It really is important to know the waters and lands from which you are harvesting foods. Talk with people in the area or the landowners. Ask agencies like your game and parks department, natural resources district, or health department about what you should be taking into account when gathering wild foods in your area.

Again, though, don't presume that you are about to enter a minefield, endangering not only yourself but also your entire family. Safety when it comes to gathering wild foods is simply a matter of knowing a few things. There are probably poisonous plants in your home; sansaveria, commonly called mother-in-law tongue or snakeweed, is a common houseplant. You most assuredly have poisons in your household cleaning supplies or in your medicine cabinet. God knows, the shelves of your local grocery store groan under the weight of dangerous, toxic materials. But you know what you are doing (hopefully!) in your home and grocery store, and that's what I'm going to help you with out in the wild. Pay attention, do what you can to learn about such things, and you'll have nothing to worry about.

I am lucky. I own a sizable piece of ground in a generally ecologically safe area of America. But I'm still cautious. I clean my harvest as carefully as I can. I stay away from the highway as surely as I avoid digging gayfeather out of cow-pies, although frankly I'd prefer the latter to the former. The bottom line is, you'd be careful about foods you get in a supermarket; be careful about foods you find in the wild.

Chapter One

BUSTED

 **Politics, n., pl. A means of livelihood
affected by the more degraded portion
of our criminal classes.**

—Ambrose Bierce, *The Devil's Dictionary*

A funny thing happened to me once on my way home from
vacation. I pulled into my driveway after a long, long drive
with a carload of annoying children and a snarly wife—not my
current one, I hasten to note—and pulled myself painfully
out of the pilot's seat of our van. Mostly just to stretch a bit
and catch a moment away from this moment of familial
bonding, I limped around the house to the front door to see
if any mail or messages had found their way to our home. A
yellow, official-looking form was taped to our front door.
Hmmm . . . I took it down and read it. I read it again. I shook
my head to clear my eyes, and I read it yet again.

No, I was not mistaken. Yes, I had read the notice cor-
rectly: My lawn had been condemned. The yellow form on

my door said I had six days to remove all "worthless vegetation" from my yard or the City of Lincoln, Nebraska, would do it for me. And charge me for the favor. The notice was clearly official, and it was signed by the City of Lincoln Weed Inspector and Grand Inquisitor. Worthless vegetation, he said. I looked around my suburban yard. What on earth could he mean by "worthless vegetation"? I saw daylilies, lamb's-quarter, dandelions, oxalis, shepherd's purse, nut grass . . . all edible, all in constant use in our kitchen. Nope, nothing worthless there.

Utterly baffled, I went into the house where the kids and wife continued their guerrilla warfare. Ignoring the familial skirmishes, I went to the telephone and called the number on the form. I was lucky: The weed inspector, Torquemada Legree, was still in his office, presumably torturing into a confession someone who'd had the temerity to tolerate crabgrass in the cracks of his sidewalk. He officiously asked for my name and the number of the citation I had found on my door. I gave it to him. He made some mumbling noises and noted that I was really playing with fire since I had only one day left to drop to my knees and surrender myself into the hands of civic authority.

I asked if he could maybe come out to my place the next day and talk with me before the deadline brought city bulldozers and napalm bombs in to clear up this problem with my lawn. He said he would be out first thing in the morning. Aha! This is the way government should work, I thought. Here is a civil servant serving a civil citizen. Say that three times as fast as you can. It's very difficult. But nothing compared with how hard it was to talk with the inspector when he showed up at our door the next morning. He came prepared for confrontation with a rebellious scofflaw, which is to say, me. I assured him that I was not trying to be a problem, I merely wanted further information about my crimes against humanity. He pointed to my daylilies in the parking area between the sidewalk and the street curb. "What about those?" he said, a hint of victory in his voice.

"Uh, those are flowers," I said. "And while flowers might be viewed as 'worthless' to some, including the City of Lincoln, they can hardly be considered useless since we ate some of that very plant for supper last night."

I could tell from the look on the Flora Sheriff's face that this was not going as he'd planned. "Okay"—I could tell he wanted to say something like *Mr. Smart-Ass*, but he didn't, yet—"what about those big leafy things over there?"

"Sour dock," I smiled. "I just picked a mess for lunch. Want to join us for a braunschweiger and sour dock sandwich?"

He didn't even smile. "What about that stuff over there?"

"Oh, my, now you have my mouth watering! That's wild garlic. And you're right, I really should throw some of those into the mix, too. But what I am wondering, sir, is what are the 'useless plants' you referred to on this form I found on my door? No kidding, I did a quick survey to see if I could figure out what you could possibly mean, and all I can find here on my property that's useless is bluegrass, and I swear to you that while there is some of that, I've done nothing to encourage it. You'd be amazed how hard it is to get rid of that stuff. You know, they just don't sell herbicides that will kill bluegrass but leave the rest of your crops—herbs, medicines, foodstuffs, and ornamentals—alone."

The Honorable Sheriff of Nottingham looked at me with contempt. "You have twenty-four hours," he said.

"Mad Dog, my attorney, will talk with you sooner than that, scurvy dog, and by the time I'm done with you, you'll wish you'd taken the time and had the brains to learn the names and uses of the plants you have just dismissed as worthless vegetation," I said, having now figured out that this was not an issue of economics, health, safety, or humor, but a matter of conscience, good sense, knowledge, and philosophy.

What's with Weeds?

Well, I won some and I lost some of the battles that followed. But mostly I won. The first thing I did was file a complaint and appeal with the City of Lincoln, noting that their personnel couldn't even identify a single weed they considered to be useless. They countered that in Lincoln, any vegetation over 6 inches high is a weed. A tree? I asked. A rosebush? Daylilies? Well, no, not those, they admitted. Those are flowers, and therefore useful. Flowers are useful? But food is not? My lawyer, Mad Dog, assured them he would dismantle them in court on a law this vague. Upon further consideration they decided that both Mad Dog and I might not be the run-of-the-mill patsies they were accustomed to when it came to matters of weed warfare and that maybe they should just let these not-even-drowsy dogs lie.

Then I found out that there was a larger problem to deal with—a County Weed Authority—and that these folks were busily spraying 2,4D (essentially Agent Orange) and diesel fuel on both sides of all our county roads, destroying wild roses, asparagus, chicory, wild strawberries—everything. It was a scorched-earth policy. The more I dug into this mess, the uglier it got, and the more uneasy the county board got as they saw a storm named Roger looming on the horizon. They announced, therefore, that they were moderating their devastation and cutting back . . . to spraying *one* side of all our county roads with 2,4D and diesel fuel!

Now, don't get me wrong, I understand that some "weed" control is necessary. But there were only four noxious weeds that were a problem in our state at that time: Canada thistle, Russian thistle, musk thistle, and leafy spurge. Not even marijuana, poison ivy, or bindweed was on that list. And they really are a problem. Neither the official policy nor the weed control processes of the City of Lincoln or County of Lancaster made any sense at all.

So I did what America used to be best at: I became involved in the democratic process. I decided to run for the Lancaster County, Nebraska, Weed Control Authority. On a pro-weed ticket. In my opening press conference, I reasoned that everyone seems to be anti-weed, so who is speaking for the weeds? Me, that's who. My campaign motto was going to be "If You Can't Beat 'Em, Eat 'Em." And when asked what I intended to do about the marijuana growing rife in the county's ditches, I blossomed into the mature politician and answered, "It should all be cut down and burned," leaving everyone from the moralists to the hippies perfectly content.

Return of the Natives

But how did this all come to pass? What was the deal with my lawn? Well, I was developing a deep interest in Native American populations in Nebraska, especially the Omaha Tribe, which has a reservation on the Missouri River about 50 miles north of the city of Omaha. I had developed a lot of friendships within the community and had even been adopted as a full-blood Omaha in September 1967. While my profession was academic folklorist, my relationship with the Omahas was not a professional connection at all but one of affection and genuine personal interest. I quickly learned that, although I was a mainstream middle-class white boy, I was far from being in a position to bring anything to them, despite their poverty and debased social status; rather, it was they who had a world to teach me. And teach me they did. My Indian friends shared everything from spiritual treasures to bits of information about native foods and medicines that they remembered from the historical past but also to some degree still pursued.

For example, one year I started to hear conversations about something called "milkweed soup." My God, I thought, we've reduced these fine people to eating milkweed, the most wretched of ditch weeds! But then I began to sense that far from being resigned to eating milkweeds, my friends were looking forward to the time the milkweed pods would be at just the right stage for harvest and cooking. Hmmm.

One friend assured me that you could buy the cheapest beef on the hoof you could find—a so-called cutter and canner—and if you cooked it with milkweed pods, the meat became a gourmet delight. Hmmm again.

At that point I started doing some nosing around in libraries, checking into edible wild plants. And somewhere along the line, I ran into this tidbit of information: You can eat milkweed, but you must be careful with it and know what you're doing because that milky sap is pretty toxic stuff—it can also be used to remove warts! The secret, I found in the books and learned later again from my Omaha friends, is to boil the young, firm pods a few minutes and then *pour off the water, which carries with it the toxic levels of the offending enzyme.* That enzyme, I also learned, is in fact the same one extracted from papayas for the manufacture of commercial meat tenderizers.

Aha! No wonder the Omahas' cheap beef was so good when cooked with milkweed! As it turns out, the Indians had been cooking their buffalo stews with meat tenderizers even while our bewildered and baffled frontier forefathers were eating rancid pork in their covered wagons!

Milkweed Soup, Corn Soup, Dried Sweet Corn

The most important thing to remember in cooking milkweed is to start with boiling water and use several changes of water in the cooking. If you start with cold water and bring the milkweed pods up to boiling, you will find a tough and bitter mess in your pot. And if you don't boil the pods, drain the water, replace with more hot water, and boil again, no matter how briefly, you may suffer ill effects from the toxic, milky sap. Don't be afraid of this; there are, after all, many domestic foods that are toxic if they are not properly prepared—rhubarb, for example—but we eat them nonetheless.

I have only cooked and eaten the young, firm pods of milkweed, but my friend Kay Young assures me that the older pods and even the flowers are also edible when prepared in this same way. Some sources also speak of eating the young shoots of milkweed, but they are so easily confused with plants like the poisonous hemp dogbane that I would rather not take the chance. I'll wait for the pods, thank you.

In my experience among the Omahas, there is a kind of standard soup with many variations that we call, generically, "Indian soup." Indian gatherings often feature soup because it's an easy way to prepare large amounts of meat easily distributed in equal amounts, which is the Indian way. Moreover, it's a traditional way of cooking, and for most cultures that's reason enough!

You simply take whatever meat you have in whatever amount you happen to have and cut it into equally sized pieces, from the size of half your thumb to your fist, depending on how opulent your feast is going to be. Add water to make soup enough to go around. Throw in whatever pasta or vegetables you happen to have or are easily and cheaply available. Our favorite Indian soup is the very ideal of simplicity: meat (usually bison, which we really like), water, corn, and perhaps a few preboiled milkweed pods—which by the way taste like artichokes, in case you wondered. (And did you know that artichokes are nothing more than large, cultivated thistles? Look at an artichoke selling for a fortune in your supermarket produce section; now take a look at a plain ol' thistle head. Amazing, no?)

I cannot bring myself to add canned corn to Indian soup. Sometimes I cut sweet corn off the cob and add it, but more often than not I dig into my larder and throw in a handful of last summer's dried sweet corn. Sweet corn is way too good to enjoy only a couple of weeks every summer, so again I turn to Indian traditions and dry up a mess of sweet corn when it's in season and on sale cheap, or even a touch late in the season when friends, neighbors, and grocery stores are trying to get rid of slightly overaged sweet corn. Since I'm going to dry it anyway, it doesn't make much difference if it has already started the aging process by sitting too long on the stalk or in the cooler.

Tie a bit of string around the stem end of a shucked ear of corn and hang it in a dry, clean place free from insects until it's totally dry on the cob. Then simply shell it by turning the ear in your hands and peeling off the dried kernels. Store in a tight container—pantry moths love sweet corn, too!—and when you are making up a batch of Indian soup, throw in a handful. You will be amazed, for the corn reconstitutes completely and tastes for all the world like fresh corn.

For another perspective on the process, a Hochunk friend of mine just sent me his own family system for drying sweet corn:

We pick the corn when the kernels are still white [Louie grows Indian blue corn at his beautiful farm home], *then put the ears in hot water and blanch them for a short period of time. Then we take the whole kernel off the cobs. Getting the corn off in whole kernels takes some time but the end product is really good. We have some dryers to use outdoors but finish the drying with an electric dryer indoors. We dry the corn until the kernels sound crunchy as you move your hand through the kernels. When you process the corn while it is still white, it will be tender when you reconstitute it. Putting up corn becomes a family affair here at the dwelling.*

It is tradition among Plains Indians for everyone at a feast to bring his or her own salt. The coffee is usually presweetened but neither the meat nor the soup is presalted. I have no idea why but I bet the origins of those customs are buried deep in tribal history and tradition. Add a pinch of salt to your bowl of bison, corn, and milkweed and you have what has to be about the best soup in the world.

Blanching

My friend uses the term *blanch* in his description of Native ways to deal with sweet corn, and blanching is a concept worth knowing when it comes to using wild plants for food, especially if you plan to put some in your freezer for later use. But there might be some confusion, because

the culinary term to *blanch* has, at least, two different meanings. This can cause problems, as you can imagine.

The problem comes up first and most for the beginning weeder with asparagus because the verb is used in both ways with this one foodstuff. Most Americans won't recognize the asparagus sold in a European market or served up in a truly European-style restaurant even in this country. We think of asparagus as yellowish green spears, full of life and vitality. But in Europe and some parts of this country (especially in the American East), asparagus is blanched as it is grown: Not long after the new spears break through the soil into the light, they are covered—with humus, soil, even artificial caps that are simply set down over the individual plants. Deprived of light, the plant thinks it's still beneath the surface of the earth, so it grows rapidly, staying tender and—what's almost creepy—never expressing the chlorophyll that gives plants their green color. So the "blanched" asparagus that's brought to your plate is white, or yellowish, very tender shoots.

Another meaning of to *blanch,* however, is to briefly steam a dish long enough to heat it through and kill whatever fungus, bacteria, bugs, or yeasts it has on it, but also to stop the natural enzymes that would otherwise work to keep it growing and maturing (and also getting tough and inedible in many cases). So if you take freshly picked wild asparagus, green and glowing with life, and you intend to freeze it, it's a good idea to "blanch" it according to meaning two: Steam it briefly to stop its enzymes before you put it into a plastic bag and drop it into the freezer.

More Native Secrets

Another time, while fishing in the Missouri River on the Omaha Reservation with some friends, I came up with a ferocious headache from the sparkling glare of the sun off the river water. My longtime tribal friend Clyde told me just to break off a willow twig growing along the bank beside us and chew on it, which he assured me would cure a headache. Hmmm. Chewing a stick will cure a headache. In later reading I found that the scientific name for the willow is *Salyx*, for concentrations of a substance called salicin prominent in the tree's inner bark. I also learned that salicin, when ingested, metabolizes to salicylic acid, otherwise known as aspirin. My Omaha friends were telling me that a good thing for a headache is an aspirin—readily available to all of us by chewing a willow stick. It's amazing what new things you can learn from old ways. "Useless vegetation" indeed!

Bringing It Home

The Omahas (later also Lakotas, Poncas, and Winnebagos) told me many such things, and I wanted to learn how to identify all the plants they were telling me about. But my teaching and family obligations in Lincoln wouldn't let me live for extended periods in the field or on the reservations where I could see and learn all these plants through the year as they sprang up, matured, and went through their various stages of growth and life. So I started bringing cuttings, seeds, and samples home to my very suburban home, and planting them around my house.

I buried large garbage cans beneath the rainspouts so I

could maintain mini swamps for cattails, sedges, arrowhead, and calamus. I soon had less and less of a conventional lawn and more and more . . . well, more and more weeds. In fact, bluegrass became something of a problem since it isn't edible or even useful. I further learned that our concept of a golf-course, monoculture-bluegrass lawn is really quite a new notion; through the years lawns have been composed of mints or herbs, or spotted with field flowers to look like a natural meadow. Nice idea, and a damn sight better for the ecology than an artificially, even futilely sustained bluegrass planting for decades, which any farmer will tell you is not a good idea at all.

Aside from my lawn being transformed from an adjunct of our home to a virtual food garden, there were benefits I had never anticipated. Of course there were the new colors of constant flowerings that bluegrass never shows and the economic benefits of mowing less, not having to fertilize, and no more worries about "pests," fungus, water, and so on, but a real surprise was the new *sounds* we had from our yard. I had never really noticed the deathly (literally!) silence of the suburbs with all their "well-tended" lawns, but it stands to reason: When you spray poisons for pests, you pretty much kill off everything else, too—the honeybees, katydids, cicadas, tree frogs . . . everything. Now every evening there was a full orchestra singing from every corner of our yard. Just that little spot of ours, unpoisoned in a landscape of sterilized lawns, had come alive—to our joy and daily pleasure.

But some of my neighbors didn't see things that way, and

so they had ratted me out to the city's lawn police, thus lead-
ing to my confrontation with civic authority and my decision to take the battle a level higher and come to open and
active support of the much-abused weed. Now, I would be
the first to admit that it wasn't going to be easy to convince
the public that a political campaign—make that "crusade"—
for a seat on something called the Lancaster County Weed
Control Authority should be taken seriously. So I didn't. I
gathered a bunch of friends around me, and we decided that
while our cause was serious, there was no reason why we
needed to be.

We decided to print up some bumper stickers and signs:
IF YOU CAN'T BEAT 'EM, EAT 'EM . . . WELSCH FOR WEED CONTROL
AUTHORITY; WELSCH FOR WEED BOARD—NOT JUST ANOTHER PRETTY
FACE; and my favorite, HONK 37 TIMES IF YOU SUPPORT WELSCH
FOR WEED BOARD. We soon found that our signs and bumper
stickers had become collector's items and were being taken
off the street as fast as we could get them out *on* the street.
So we started selling them to get campaign funds to print
more.

Ah yes, the blood and bones of American politics—fund-
raising! We needed some money, if for nothing else then for
what was clearly going to be a victory party when the elec-
tions were over. One of my campaign managers, the afore-
mentioned attorney, to wit: "Mad Dog," had some ideas, one
of which was actually legal, mostly. We had a mutual friend
and campaign supporter who offered us his palatial home
for a fund-raising dinner. We would use his grand lawn,
sweeping down to a charming lakefront. And we would con-

tinue the humble spirit of our campaign by serving beans and wienies for 99 cents a plate. Isn't that what the big-time political campaigners do in America? Sort of?

Corruption Creeps into the Campaign

But Mad Dog had another idea, too: We could really boost our net at the fund-raiser by also selling beer for 99 cents a glass out of a keg. "Uh . . . " I felt a bit silly asking an attorney about the niceties of the law, but I did it anyway: "Uh, Steve . . . isn't it illegal to sell beer without a license?"

"Don't worry," he said. "I'll take care of it."

Believe it or not, that gave me enormous confidence because in the past he had always taken care of it. Often in remarkably inventive ways, but yes, he had always taken care of whatever scrapes I had gotten myself into—or he had gotten me into, for that matter.

The night of the party was glorious. The weather was perfect. A friend had baked up a huge mess of truly wonderful beans and wienies. The beer was cold and the kegs stood ready on the patio. "Are you sure we aren't going to get into trouble by selling beer illegally, Steve?" I asked Mad Dog one last time. "I mean, this could really wreck our campaign, what with ethics and all."

"Ah yes," Mad Dog guffawed. "But ethics aside . . ." My confidence was shaken.

It shouldn't have been. I was at the door greeting my supporters as they came in and watching the money flow into the till as the beer flowed into the paper cups when down the line of guests came—oh, my God!—the county attorney. And his staff. I swallowed deep and held my arms out to be cuffed. But the law enforcers weren't there to arrest me for selling beer without a license—they were there because Mad Dog had given everyone in the county attorney's office free tickets to the grand event, and being themselves politicians, they saw this as one of the biggest events of the county's election season, so here they were: at a gathering where the laws against selling beer without a license, laws they had sworn to uphold, were being openly violated. But—well, they were at the party themselves! What could they do? Bust themselves?

The county attorney looked around and laughed when he realized how he had been flimflammed into participating in an illegal gathering—and, relieved to see the boss laugh, all his deputies laughed, too.

"Okay, you guys, you got us this time," he said. "But exactly one hour from the time we finish our meal, have a couple of beers, and leave this party, the sheriff will be at the door to check for violations of the Lancaster County liquor laws." And that's precisely what happened. The county attorney left, the sheriff and some deputies arrived shortly thereafter, and all they found was a bunch of tired and tipsy political workers cleaning up the rubble from what had clearly been a lovely party. Nothing wrong with that. No rules broken there.

On the Road to Victory

Well, that wasn't the first, biggest, or last remarkable anecdote to come out of my first political campaign. The best was yet to come. Utterly unbeknownst to me, the CBS writer, host, and reporter, a real hero of mine, Charles Kuralt came through Nebraska on one of his national swings, taping stories for his then-new series, *On the Road with Charles Kuralt*. He was in Grand Island, Nebraska, not far from where I now live, and he was speaking to the Nebraska Press Association, as the story was later told to me. While he was eating at the head table, he asked one of the people sitting with him, naturally enough, if they happened to know of anything going on in Nebraska that might make a good *On the Road* story— you know, something a bit zany, human interest, something with a bit of a twist to it, what journalists and other writers refer to as "The Hook."

To this day I don't know who the person beside Kuralt was at that banquet, but heaven knows I owe him big, because he said, "Well, yeah. There is this crackpot in Lincoln who's running for the county weed board . . . on a pro-weed ticket." Kuralt called me the next morning, putting our household into a froth, and we arranged to serve supper that very day to a media man of national stature. When he parked that big CBS van out in front of our house, he caused quite a stir throughout the entire neighborhood, as you can imagine. But not as much of a stir as that single day would have in my life.

Kuralt became a fast and steady friend for the next twenty-five years, and what's more, so did the members of the crew he had with him on that trip—his best friend and cinematographer, Izzy Bleckman, and soundman Larry Gianneschi. Both later became my own crew when I started to doing essays for Charles on his great show *CBS News Sunday Morning*. And when Larry retired, his son Danny became my sound technician and dear friend, too. Little did I know that day that I was going to acquire a completely new family and totally different direction in my life. See what growing weeds and not mowing your lawn can do for you?

Over the years Kuralt did six or seven more of his *On the Road* shows with me featuring one thing or another I was doing, and as I said, eventually he put me on *Sunday Morning* as an essayist. But on this occasion, he nailed down my political career. Here I was, running for an utterly insignificant county committee seat, and I was getting national coverage. You can imagine what that will do to a traditional campaign! On the night of the election, I was driving from one party and heading to another when the polls closed. I think it was at 8:00 P.M. At 8:05 the announcer on my car radio said, "Well, it's way too early to make any predictions, I suppose, but I think we can project, with two precincts reporting, that Roger Welsch is going to be a landslide victor in his race for Lancaster County Weed Control Authority."

Later that evening, at a victory party, a reporter told me that in many precincts I was getting more votes than popular and successful Nebraska politician Jim Exon was getting in his run for the U.S. Senate in that same election. "What do you think of that?" the reporter asked me.

"Well," I said, not without justification, "it's just a damn good thing Jim wasn't running run for the weed board." And that is why, to this day, I am known by some as "Landslide" Welsch. At least I think that's why they call me "Landslide."

I won't bore you with much more of this story, but I served two terms on the Weed Authority, making friends and allies of many of the veteran Authority members, help- ing elect other progressive and concerned members, and completely changing around county policy, continuing to control noxious weeds but not in ways that wreaked such havoc with everything else growing alongside. In fact, we were eventually so successful that the county commission- ers killed and eliminated the Lancaster County Weed Con- trol Authority because we were getting way too much attention, getting way too many things done, doing way too good a job . . . and thus making them look really bad since they were mostly hapless dimbulbs.

Their rationale for eliminating the weed board was the standard canard of "budget cutting." We commissioners were paid something like $12 a month. So these geniuses got rid of a panel of seven trained and dedicated experts who were doing heroic work and costing them virtually nothing and instead started making all weed control decisions on their own, based on total ignorance and costing the county a fortune. Sadly, that, too, is a traditional part of American politics, I guess.

So that's how I got here to where I am vis-à-vis weeds and you and this book. I got here by having a messy lawn. And by enjoying the bounty nature gives us.

Chapter Two

WHAT'S FOR SUPPER?

In al gardeins,
Some flowers,
Some weedes . . .

—John Lyly, 1579

Don't make the mistake I made upon hearing that my Omaha Indian friends were about to scour the reservation ditches for milkweed. I'm not suggesting that you eat something distasteful, or even simple survival fare. Life is too short to eat stuff you don't like. As I did with Charles Kuralt and his crew the first time they came to my table, in these pages I intend to serve you up a menu of real delicacies, a gourmet feast. As I wrote in my book about men and food, *Diggin' In and Piggin' Out*, while we all tend to think that we eat what's edible, and maybe even everything that's edible, it's not quite that simple. Neither do we eat what we eat because it tastes particularly good, because it's convenient, because it's economical, because it's nutritious . . . We eat what we eat because that's what we eat. It's habit and tradition, plain and simple.

We eat what we eat, in large part, because of deep cultural and personal meanings that food happens to have for us—but the key word there is *happens*. The circumstances are not universal: What we eat for breakfast would send a lot of peoples of the world into paroxysms of retching. Eggs, bacon, coffee, cheese omelet with shredded beef—you can't imagine what those foods that have me drooling can conjure up by way of disgust in the minds of some people!

Same with weeds. My parents once returned home from a vacation trip to Hawaii. Knowing my interest in native foods, they brought me a jar of "poha jelly." They told me this rare and expensive jelly is made from berries growing on South Seas island mountain slopes . . . a real gourmet treat. I tried it. Hmmm . . . tastes familiar, I thought. Yep, I recognized the taste of that "poha." It was ground cherries. Plain old Japanese lantern, pop berry, ground cherries. Like those growing outside the back door steps at my parents' home. Here it's a troublesome weed; on a tourist shop counter, it is a rare and expensive, exotic and elegant native berry.

In the mostly highly rated restaurant I have ever eaten in, in the English countryside, the elegant vegetable I was served was labeled "oyster root." Around here we know it as meadow salsify. Grows everywhere. Here, a pest; there, a delicacy. See how it works? I think my son Chris said it best, but inadvertently, when he once came in to the table for supper, looked somewhat surprised at the iceberg lettuce

Ground Cherries

I'm not much of a cook—my expertise lies in eating—so not many of the "recipe sidebars" in these pages will deal with cooking. Yes, ground cherries—small orange fruits similar in size and shape to cherry tomatoes, covered in papery husk—can be cooked up in jams and jellies (see chapter 8), but to my mind and taste the best way to consume ground cherries is to pick 'em and eat 'em. Ground cherries belong to the same family as tomatoes: the, uh, deadly nightshade family. And just as tomatoes had for centuries the reputation of being poisonous, some people see ground cherries as merely suitable for children to squash as "pop berries"—they certainly wouldn't pick one off the vine and eat it!

I have had some queasiness from eating *green* ground cherries, but once they have turned a golden yellow, I have found only pleasure in them. You peel away the papery outer sheath, which looks like the Chinese lanterns you buy for lawn parties and is what makes these fruits fun for children to pop between their hands, and inside you find a golden nugget that has a very pleasant tomatoey taste. I suppose you could cook them . . . but why go to the trouble?

salad in a large bowl in the center of the table, and asked in all seriousness, "What's the matter, Dad? Are we out of weeds?" I'll have more to say about meadow salsify later.

Caveat Eater

Which is not to say that after reading this book you're going to be able to go out and graze at random in roadside ditches. Imagine turning a Native fresh from the Brazilian rain forest loose into an American supermarket to find his supper. He wouldn't have any idea what's potato chips and what's roach paste, drain cleaner and garlic powder, dish sponges and ice cream. That could be a very dangerous state of innocence.

Same with us when looking at the bounty of the country-side. Some weeds are deadly poisons. Some that are poisonous at one stage are fine to eat at another, or maybe a dangerous plant can be made benign by preparing it in a certain way, or even one part of a plant can be a delicacy while another part just up or down the stem is deadly poison. Did you know rhubarb leaves and roots are poisonous? Yep, but the stems are perfectly delicious, especially when baked in a pie. It's just that the leaves and roots are poison.

I have often wondered about how we human beings have come to know what is edible and what isn't. Insofar as we do know that sort of thing. There is still some question, you know. The quite attractive vining plant commonly called deadly nightshade is obviously poisonous—why else call it "deadly"—and is widely considered to be so even by people who are fairly naive when it comes to plant identification. Except by those who bake the plant's dark, almost black berries up into pies and eat them. And that dichotomy, much like the one about the toxic-or-not nature of the "love apple," aka the tomato, has raged for centuries. But I'm not about to eat something called "deadly" and long thought to be poisonous. Are you? Still, I wonder about all those people who smack their lips when they talk about the nightshade pie—with ice cream no less—that they had for dessert the night before. In that same nightshade family is that plant that similarly had long been thought to be deadly poison—the tomato. And then some guy who didn't know the facts ate one, liked it, and invented pizza and catsup.

My point is that there are plants that have a reputation for being poisonous that are nonetheless eaten. Or even more to the point, there's a lot we don't know about our gastrobotany yet, and we therefore need to exercise caution. Playing with fire or missing some great pie? This question is most certainly part of the reason some people eat things that others consider disgusting or dangerous: We are still in the process of learning what foods are safe and/or good. After all, there are still some Americans who don't seem to understand where babies come from.

Peasant under Glass

There is also the societal dimension of food. A neighbor, when I lived the cursed life of suburbia, once asked me what this whole thing between me and weeds was about. I told him that I liked the idea of wild foods and that a lot of the things growing right there in his yard were as good as the kinds of things he was buying at the grocery store. I pointed to the garden he was working in and told him that the sour dock he was hoeing out between the rows was easily as tasty as and a lot more nutritious than the lettuce he was trying to grow in the rows. He looked at me with just a hint of contempt and snarled, "I ain't about to eat no goddamn weed."

Sour Dock

Don't let that name put you off. Yes, dock is tangy, zesty, tart, and maybe even sour to your palate, but there's a reason people put oil and *vinegar* dressing on salads—to give it some interest to the taste buds. Dock can do that for you in the wild. As always, try to find young, tender leaves. They may be the center leaves in a cluster of older, tougher leaves, so don't give up just because all you see at first glance are mature plants. Wash the leaves and tear them into manageable pieces just as you would do with any salad green. Mix these tangy greens in with blander lettuce or spinach, or in the wild with purslane, and your salad will come with its own naturally vinegary dressing!

Sour dock is also an excellent green for a "potherb," or cooked green. Spinach can be eaten green and fresh as a salad ingredient or cooked as a vegetable—same with dock. Boil or steam fresh young greens for just a short time. Don't reduce the leaves to ropy gobs, which seems to be the way most people think of spinach. And just as a few drops of lemon spice up a bland cooked green in the kitchen, in the wild dock comes along with its own touch of tart. Add a little bacon grease or butter, and some salt, to your pot of dock and you will have a first-rate, and very wholesome, vegetable green to go along with your T-bone steak from the campfire.

A not inconsiderable advantage of dock is that it's one of the first green things you see in the spring and one of

> the last in the autumn. While the older leaves do get tough, leathery, and woody, there are always young, tender leaves at the center of the crown. As I write these words, it is late October. We have had frost and at least one hard freeze, and yet I note that all around I see bright and fresh sour dock looking just as lively as it did six months ago. Clearly, sour dock is an edible worth remembering!

And I was enormously pleased at that moment that I had been spared developing that same kind of cultural myopia myself. Our pioneer forefathers, for all the praise they get in history lessons for their ingenuity, adaptability, and courage, were actually pretty stupid by and large. They weren't about to eat no goddamn Indian food. So instead, they starved, ate terrible food, got sick, and suffered far more than they needed to. In some cases here on the Plains, settlers reverted to "Indian food"—jerked meat, ground nuts, wild tubers and berries—during times of imminent starvation, even commenting in journals and diaries that these "Indian foods" were really quite good, even delicious! But as soon as they could, the pioneers abandoned those victuals in favor of good, honest, decent white man's food. And went back to sickness and starvation.

I revel in eating not only unlikely or exotic foods but also poor people's food. Not out of some kind of self-sacrifice or political symbolism, but because it tends to be good food. Okay, it's true, my family is thoroughly and notably (and in my case, unapologetically) peasant stock. For centuries they were the bottom of the social and economic structure, outcasts and immigrants, oddballs and intruders. It didn't help that they also tended to be arrogant and obnoxious, but that's another issue. What matters here is that they had excellent food.

Not expensive food. *Good* food. In fact, they had to settle for the worst of food—that's the lot of the poor. But here's the thing: The poor who get the worst portions of whatever there is to eat therefore have to develop ever-more-refined procedures for making it good. The rich don't have to do that. What is harder to make taste good—prime loin of beef or that same cow's head? What offers itself up to better eating—a pork chop or that same pig's intestines? Obviously, it takes a lot more skill to make an edible dish out of the second of each of those choices. The first is a snap. The rich folks get the first, the poor get the latter.

And yet both pieces of meat in both cases are from the same animal, right? Same animal, same meat. What's different is the level of skill in the cooking. And the poor folks far and away have the process of making the lowly taste good down pat. Sausage, cracklings, ribs, pork rinds, menudo, tacos, on and on and on . . . delicious delicacies made by the poor from the kitchen discards of the rich. This is why the foods of the British Isles have such a dreadful reputation: People go to England, Scotland, or Ireland and head for a fancy restaurant. The food is terrible. The recipes are rich people's recipes. Anyone can screw up a tenderloin.

But go to an English country tavern instead. Eat what those

dirty laborers are eating over there in the corner—yeah, the ones who are already half drunk and singing bawdy songs. Pasties, bubble and squeak, bangers and mash, ploughman's lunch . . . I told you. Delicious, right? That's because it's *real* English food, food from the lower classes, made delicious by a cook's skill rather than the options of wealth.

Same with weeds. You can pay big money for iceberg lettuce and might just as well be eating chilled typing paper. Or you can eat the products of the ditches and fields and eat well and healthy. Again—far from suggesting that you eat something that tastes bad, in these pages I am going to offer you paths to much better munching than you are used to.

What's Where? What's What?

Another variable in any discussion of edible wild foods is the very real consideration that not everything grows everywhere. That should be obvious, perhaps, but we sometimes forget how huge this nation, this world, even some states are and that over relatively short distances, plant distributions change dramatically. I live in Nebraska, for example, and I can't even give a generalized presentation of what is edible and available from one end of this state to the other—a distance of 400 miles. In those miles one goes from the deep hardwood forests along the Missouri River bottoms to arid sand deserts of our state's panhandle region. You can readily find pokeweed in Nebraska City in the east . . . but not in Alliance in the west. You can find prickly pear cactus even here in my fields in the dead center of the state, but not 100 miles to the east.

So while I will indeed talk about some specific plants in this book, you would do well to understand that what I'm familiar with in my own region may be totally different elsewhere, even just a few miles away. The idea here is the idea . . . the idea of learning about and using wild plants in any area. Different plants, but the same idea.

Nor am I going to try to describe plants to you so you can identify them. You need to find a book specifically designed for that purpose, specifically targeted to your geographic location. Go the library, or the bookstore, or the Web. Those resources are out there. Better yet, as you will read in these pages over and over again, find a person who can show you what plants are what. The only sure way to know what you're looking at, after all, is to look at it. Once you see a plant and know its name, you are not likely to forget it. On the other hand, if you try to figure out what a plant is by following a key through a description of the indentations on its leaves, the relative length of the stems, the subtle coloration of its flowers, the complicated structure of its fruit, well, that's just not the best, easiest, or surest way to do it.

Hang on. It gets worse. Even as the variety of plants differs from mile to mile across our land, north to south as well as east to west, so, too, do the names applied to those plants. I'm not a scientist, but I suppose I should have learned all the unambiguous scientific labels for all the plants I know and love and that I talk about in these pages. But no, I still call it sour dock, shepherd's purse, and pigweed, knowing full well that what one person calls pigweed may not be what I am thinking of as pigweed at all. I suppose I like common names because of the romance—ah, pigweed!—and maybe I've just been lazy in not learning the "proper" scientific labels.

Well, I'll try to provide the scientific labels where I can, but you can be sure that in conversation I'm still going to use the common name. Again, it's a matter of what my real message is in these pages. I'm not trying to tell you that in Lincoln, Nebraska, you can probably still find pokeweed scattered around the campus of Nebraska Wesleyan University, where I found my supply forty years ago; my intention is to encourage you to keep in mind that *something* good is within a few yards of where you are sitting reading this right now, whether you're on a bus in Washington, D.C., or sitting horseback heading toward a trout stream near Florissant, Colorado.

That little toss-off line is more fact than you might imagine. I was indeed once walking down a street with a friend who was asking me about my interest in edible wild plants. She noted that since she had a job in downtown Baltimore, Maryland, this obviously wasn't an interest she was going to be able to enjoy with me. For the next hundred steps or so I pointed out to her the edible wild plants I spotted along the curb, in abandoned window boxes, by doorsteps, in alleyways, growing from cracks in the sidewalk.

Now, to be sure—to be damn sure!—I'd want to be a lot more cautious about washing any plants I harvested from cracks in a Baltimore sidewalk. But the plants are there. And I'm betting it wouldn't take much effort to find a good, fresh, nutritious salad in a place a touch farther removed from hacking winos and peeing house pets, even in Baltimore. (Which reminds me: Can anyone tell me why people are going hungry in our cities even while all those fat pigeons are sitting right there on their windowsills? They look a lot like Cornish hens to me.)

Actually, to be perfectly honest, it's not just that city people are ignorant of the plants that flourish under their very eyes. I know plenty of people who live in open, rural areas of America and drive down highways flanked by great open fields, pastures, parks, and wildernesses who haven't the faintest notion of what all that green and what all those blooms around them are. I know that because I was once one of those people. To me it was all a matter of "green," with occasional splashes of white, yellow, maybe some blue. Weeds, I'm sure I thought.

That's not a good way to go through life, ignorant of what's around us. Even if you don't intend to eat the plants and flowers you see, shouldn't you at least do all those things of beauty the courtesy of knowing their names? You will be amazed, if you join me in this adventure, at what a different aspect the countryside, a casual drive through it, or for that matter life itself takes on when you know what it is you're looking at. No longer will you suffer long boring trips through eternal hours endless miles away to get to family reunions or business gatherings with nothing to see—nothing at all!—but empty roadsides and wastelands. "My God, this trip gets longer every time we drive it. I am bored to tears. How much farther is it now? Oh man . . . another hour of this dreariness?"

Nope, now your trips will be a matter of "Wow! Is the blue of that chicory spectacular this morning, or what? We should come back here in October and dig some up for our coffee."

"Look at all those white blossoms—we have to remember this place next July when those chokecherries are ready for picking! Chokecherry soup . . . oh, man, makes my mouth water just thinking of it."

"I don't see them yet, but that perfume is unmistakable—elderberries! Let's stop and pick some for tea."

"Isn't that an old asparagus brush by that fence? It's late April—that stuff should be coming up soon. Let's stop for just a second and see if there aren't some juicy fresh spears ready for a quick lunch!" This is truly the kind of thing that happens when you live *with* the world around you and get to know it. It becomes a different place. And what's more, a fascinating place.

Weeds and the Alpha Male

I may be revealing far too much about myself at this point, but I know that deep down weeds fulfill some sort of primal male urge. Or maybe adolescent male urge. My wife, Linda, would argue that that's redundant. I wrote a book about love, sex, and marriage once and thought that I'd given away so many secrets about men, we should market it in a plain brown paper bag with the words prominently displayed, FOR SALE TO WOMEN ONLY WITH THE WRITTEN PERMISSION OF AN ADULT MALE! To which my Lovely Linda mumbled, "And just where are we supposed to find one of those?"

But okay, we're adults here. Let's be honest. Men are at heart boys, and boys—children in general—love the idea of free food that can be picked right off the stem and eaten even as you walk along a path or through a woodland.

Heaven knows, that's the way I feel about it. And you have to admit it: If you've ever had anything to do with a kid or a man, there is a certain kinship that cannot be denied by the participants or the observer.

So where do you start with your quest for wild foods? You look out your car window at the passing scenery or even out your back window at the weeds growing along the alley and behind your garage and you say to yourself, "Man . . . that's a big wide world o' wild weeds out there! And they all look alike." You pick up a book on plant identification, and you see 300 pages of technical descriptions, Latin phrases, scientific terminology—you're never going to learn all this stuff. It's easier to go to the grocery store, you're thinking, and let the guy who runs the produce counter tell you what he has and how to eat it.

The thing is, you don't memorize everything on every shelf of every aisle the first time you go shopping in a grocery store, and the same is true for foraging for wild foods. Find someone congenial who knows about wild foods or simply plants of your region and have this friend show you and tell you about one or two plants. Try them. Prepare them for the table in a couple of different ways. Don't try anything else until you are certain about how you feel about these one or two plants, and you are absolutely certain you'll never mistake—not ever—sour dock for wooly mullein, which is not edible. Then go to your friend and tell him or her you're ready for your next lesson.

Start with common plants—they're the most useful and they will give you the most opportunities to eat them and revel in your new knowledge—maybe even show it off to someone who doesn't even know one edible wild food.

The Humble Lion's Tooth

Start with something you already know. If you have any savvy at all about weeds, if you have ever tried to groom a suburban lawn, if you were ever a kid, you know about dandelions. Well, there's your start. Dandelion greens picked before the plant flowers are mild, loaded with vitamins, easily found, and a delightful addition to any salad. See? There you are. You are already identifying and eating wild foods!

But don't stop there. If you like interesting, light wines, you can make pretty good household wine out of dandelion flowers. And while you're digging up those pesky rascals from your lawn, save the roots, roast them in your oven until they're baked hard and start showing just a touch of smoke, and then grind them for an interesting addition to your morning coffee—a bit like chocolate, not unlike chicory, the roots of which are also roasted and added to coffee in many parts of the world.

Dandelions, like cattails, are a veritable grocery store in and of themselves. Not to mention one of the prettiest flowers I know. I cannot understand at all the animosity some people seem to have for dandelions. I am also fond of them because every so often around here, in what seems to be the very bowels of winter—December, January, even February in the ferocious cold of the northern Plains—there it will be: that incredibly cheery yellow glow. I cannot imagine what brings a dandelion to bloom at a time like that, but I always welcome it when it does.

Dandelion Wine

A lot is said of dandelion wine, but I think it's more poetry than delicacy. It's an awful lot of work for what amounts to a passable wine. It takes a full gallon of dandelion flowers—only the yellow part, no green whatsoever—and that's a lot of picking. Still, if you must:

Pour a gallon of hot water over the gallon of flowers and add three pounds of sugar. Stir until the sugar is completely dissolved. Add a teaspoon of wine yeast nutrient if you have it and commercial wine yeast once the mixture cools; two handfuls of raisins can provide a decent yeast source albeit a poor substitute for the commercial wine yeast. Add two full teaspoons of wine acid blend (available from any winemaker's supply store) or the juice of two lemons and two oranges—more if you prefer a tart wine. Let the wine ferment a few days on the flowers, stirring a couple of times a day to be sure the flowers are covered. Then strain off the liquor. Keep in a crock until the wine is completely fermented (when the bubbling and frothing stops and the brew becomes still), and has started to settle or become clear, then transfer to closed containers for a final aging.

Dandelion roots heated to smoking make a passable morning drink. I hesitate to call it coffee because (1) it isn't really coffee, and (2) to me it tastes more like a light chocolate. The crown of a dandelion—the blanched base bulb between the root and leaves—is a decent vegetable, and the leaves are a prized green, but be sure you gather and eat the crown or greens before the plant flowers. At that point the plant takes on a bitter, milky sap that isn't at all pleasant. Not long ago we had steamed dandelion greens with some crowns, topped with a bit of hot bacon grease and sunflower seeds. Delicious.

One of my campaign mottos when I ran for the weed board was "If You Can't Beat 'Em, Eat 'Em," and that certainly applies to dandelions. If you feel driven to destroy dandelions, why not do it by serving them up on a plate? A neighbor of mine was once driven almost to distraction because he was constantly beset by (1) dandelions in his lawn, and (2) cottontail rabbits eating his flowers and gardens. I on the other hand did nothing at all to "care" for my lawn, and I had no problems at all. The answer was simple enough, but I didn't have the heart to tell him. I had cottontails in my yard every morning and evening, too. I enjoyed watching them. I watched them eat . . . the flowers from my dandelions. I had no dandelion flowers and only a few dandelions because I had bunnies. He had tons of dandelion flowers because he chased away his weeders.

Chapter Three
THINK FOOD

Shall I not also rejoice at the abundance of weeds, whose seeds are the granaries of the birds?

—Henry David Thoreau

If you've ever spent any time at all fishing, skinny-dipping, wading in a creek, camping by a river, or hiking the country-side, you probably can identify cattails, a plant not easily mistaken for anything else in this world. Cattails are common almost everywhere. And they are a virtual grocery store in one plant, at just about any time of year, not to mention that they make excellent weapons for impromptu sandbar fights. Nothing beats the explosion of a cattail head when it is firmly planted with a full swing against someone else's fanny.

My friend Rolly Brennick and I were once camped with a couple of our own kids and a huge passel of other people's kids on the banks of the Missouri River somewhere down below the Fort Randall dam. The section of river had just been opened and approved as a merit badge project for young canoers, and we were inaugurating the float. It was a gorgeous float on a river so crystal clear you could see 6 to 8 feet down in the water, the dam above us catching and hold- ing all the silt that turns the river into the "Muddy Mo" above and below this stretch. Camps were set up all around us—a couple hundred young boys—and a mess station was being set up for supper. But Rollie and I and our kids were ready for a snack, and as we'd been floating along I'd been lecturing, as I tend to do, about wild foods we were seeing along the bank—like Cossack asparagus. The boys thought we should quickly cook up a mess just for fun and snacking.

So I walked down to a little backwater with Rollie and the kids, a couple of others from neighboring fireplaces joining us. I waded into the shallow water and over to a cattail patch, where I showed the kids how easy it is to reach down to the base of a stalk and pull up, easily breaking the stalk loose. I cut away the top leaves and peeled off the tougher outer sheath. I cut away a few sections and tasted them to be sure they were ready to eat. And they were just fine, to my taste like a combination of cantaloupe and watermelon with a touch of cucumber. Instantly the boys wanted to taste, too. It wasn't what they were used to, of course, so some liked it, some didn't. But they all liked the idea of eating something right out of the river.

More boys from the larger camp joined us in the marsh. We pulled up more cattails. I told them to gather with care and we would do little damage to the enormous colony of cattails. Soon we were surrounded by husks and leaves, and we were all eating and commenting on this new and curious food. "But don't get all filled up on the raw stuff," I cautioned. "Frankly, I like it better cooked!" We gathered a mess of stalks and carried them over to our tents and campfire. We dug out as big a pot as we had—not big enough—and one of the boys ran over to the mess tent and got a bigger pot, to the grumbling of the resident cook who was planning something fresh out of the plastic package—you know, something nutritious and hygienic.

Then I taught the boys a trick I had learned from my Indian friends. For one thing, we had built our fire of cottonwood and ash. Cottonwood doesn't throw sparks—a very important advantage for Indians camped in tipis or earth lodges and sleeping close to the fire! And ash burns well dry and cured *or* green and wet, while throwing down great coals for cooking.

But that wasn't my big trick. There are at least two kinds of fires. First, there's the campfire—you know, the one you sit around and stare into and tell stories around and sip cold whiskey by? And then there's a cooking fire. These are not the same. You sure don't want to be cooking over a rising flame, or having people constantly moving around you while you're cooking, kicking sand into the food, wanting to sample it, giving you free advice you don't want or need. So at the tents you build a nice big fire to sit around and stare into, for warmth and comfort. And then you use a shovel to carry a few coals to a little pit you've set up elsewhere in camp. That's your cooking fire—not too hot, not smoky, not clogged up by socializing, nowhere near the activities that are inevitable in a camp.

I dug a small trench, filled it with coals, set the big pot

across it, and filled it with water. We cleaned the stalks and cut them up into inch-long pieces. When the water was about to boil, we threw in the cattail sprouts. I added some bacon grease saved from our breakfast pans for just such an occasion, along with a dash of salt. Moments later I took the bubbling pot off the cooking fire and signaled everyone to bring a plate and fork. And soon I had a long line of young scouts abandoning the official mess tent and digging into this strange stuff the weird guys were cooking over at the edge of the camp—something called Cossack asparagus, but really plain ol' cattails . . . you know, *weeds*! Even the boys who weren't all that crazy about the taste ate their share— they wanted to go home and tell their buddies about eating *weeds*. And each of the following nights, Rollie and I worked at cooking up messes of cattails, greens, salads, and mint teas from wild foods we found along the river.

There's just something about weeds and kids.

Supermarkets of the Swamp

Of all the foodstuffs that cattails offer, my favorite is the fresh young shoots—the so-called Cossack asparagus—in early spring. These make the easiest way to eat cattails, too: Pull up the young stalks, peel off a couple of layers of the outer, tougher leaves . . . and eat. Shoots can be cut up and added to a salad, or boiled (or better, steamed) for a few minutes, seasoned with salt, bacon grease, or butter, and served.

Soon after the shoots appear, the cattail plant sends up its characteristic tall flower stalk and begins to form the "cattail" itself. While most people who have noticed the plant at all along riversides, lakesides, and marshes have seen the dark brown cylinders that form the seed head of the plant—there's always a red-winged blackbird sitting on it, kind of like a garnish—before that head becomes brown, dry, and hard, it is smaller and green, and edible! While the head is green in color, perhaps with a thin brown stripe up one side, it's as edible and nutritious as sweet corn. You may need a sharp knife or cutters to detach the head without breaking it open.

Green cattail heads are prepared by dropping them into salted boiling water for about five to ten minutes until tender. They never get soft tender but remain al dente—firm but edible. As with corn on the cob, a dab of butter or bacon grease really improves cattail on the cob, which tends to be a bit drier than ear corn at any rate.

But as they say in those annoying television ads, "But wait! There's more!" Once the cattail is a week or so older, it flowers. That cylindrical cattail is the female part of the flower, but there appears from the top a plume heavily laden with abundant yellow pollen, as edible as pancake flour. The pollen is easy collected by pulling a paper or plastic bag over the head—you will find that the pollen is already shaking off freely and generously—and then give the bagged head a good shake. Move from head to head with your sack and you will soon find that you have more than enough to stretch your breakfast pancake mix or evening biscuit dough a long way. Pick out any stray bugs that might have been on the cattail head (or not) and mix the golden flour in with whatever biscuit, bread, or pancake flour you brought along with you.

And when all else is gone, when autumn has apparently removed all the edible foods from the landscape, there is still the cattail in the marsh. It may be a cold and mucky business, but in a pinch it's worth your while to dig out the ropy roots underlying the cattail marsh. Because when you peel off the tough outer wrapping, inside the root you will find whitish, woody strands encased in loose flakes of starch. The cattail plant has stored these flakes for its winter survival or spring revival—or your survival. Don't worry about being cruel to cattails. They are scarcely an endangered species, and in digging up the roots for your ingestion, you're likely spreading the plant more than you are damaging it.

Preparing cattail roots for eating is complicated, however, as is the gathering. I would definitely put cattail root flour in the category of an emergency food because it involves so much work for a little return. Plan on getting your hands dirty: You cannot pull the roots up by the stalk. You need to dig them up from the muck. Rinse the roots and peel them. Pull off the tough external "bark." Rinse the starch flakes out from within the fibrous strands of the root, spreading the fibers, shaking, and rinsing out as much as you can. You want to get as much return for your work as possible. Strain and rinse the flakes and let them settle in clean water. The flakes at the bottom are your product. They will provide the basic flour for the best buckwheat pancakes you've ever eaten—although maybe their deliciousness is just that you are so hungry and cold from the work you went through to get the stuff! As with so much wild food, if you can, try using your wild "flours" like cattail root starch or pollen as a stretcher for what milled wheat flour you might have in your larder. Mix the wild product about half and half with the commercial and use as you would pancake batter.

Another plan is simply to boil up the whole root as you pull it from the swamp and then chew it to extract the starch, spitting out the fibers. It's pretty indelicate, but in a survival situation delicacy and etiquette will probably be your last consideration.

Now and then in these pages I'm going to tell you some things about wild plants that have nothing to do with eating, and, I suppose have nothing much to do with anything at the bottom line. "Bottom line . . ." Hahahahahahahaha! Sometimes I knock myself out. See, the thing is, cattail leaves were woven for floor mats for Kickapoo Indian lodges. The Pilgrims at Plimoth Plantation used cattail stems to thatch the roofs of their huts. But to my mind the most ingenious use of cattail was that of the Omaha Tribe, which created disposable diapers from it. That's right: While our white ancestors were pooping in their streams and wells, the savages on this continent were using hygienic, disposable diapers in their tents and wickiups!

Indian lodges often housed whole families or clans. Omaha earth lodges might have thirty or forty people living under one roof. Old folks, young marrieds, single folks . . . and children. Including babies. And Indian babies were just as irresponsible about their, uh, "leavings" as modern kids are. And you just cannot have a toddler dropping poop in the house wheresoever he feels the inclination, if you catch my drift, especially if your house is an unlit earth lodge. So

Omaha lodges were furnished with large bags made of soft deerskin. During the summer and fall, women gathered cattail heads, broke them open (they almost explode in a puff of very soft, fluffy down), and stuffed the fluff into the bags. Now they had big, soft lounging chairs for their lodges, for all the world like beanbag chairs.

And they made soft deerskin diapers for their babies. During the winter, when everyone was indoors sheltered from the ferocity of Plains weather, the diapers were put loosely on a child; Mom reached into one of the lounging chairs, took out a generous handful of the downy cattail fluff, and lined the leather outer case with it. When the child soiled his diaper, Mom simply took the diaper off Junior's heinie, shook out the beshatted cattail fluff lining somewhere away from the lodge, relined the diaper with cattail fluff, and put it back on Junior. By the time spring came, the bag chairs were empty and ready for the new year's supply of fresh, clean cattail fluff. Ingenious, no?

Weed Rule #1: There Are No Weed Rules

Getting to know wild foods isn't at all a tough assignment. If you learn to identify only a couple of common trees, get to know a few of the showiest flowers, learn just one or two of the most common edible plants that grow in every yard and garden, you will find that you can fascinate children by actually finding something to eat at their front sidewalk. Why, they saw those things every day as they went to school and never once suspected that . . .

When you're beginning to look at wild foods, begin as broadly as you can. Learn to identify and prepare for the palate some plants for each season. Again, things like cattails are great for this because they provide fare throughout the year. But consider morel mushrooms and asparagus for the early spring, dock and dandelions, poke and mulberries for late spring, sumac, plums, and chokecherries for summer, rose hips and ground cherries for late summer, Jerusalem artichokes and arrowhead for autumn . . . You don't have to learn immediately enough to live on, just enough to enjoy the countryside through the seasons.

Start (maybe even stick) with what interests you. There are no written requirements, rules, or standards of performance when it comes to eating weeds! If you are interested in berries but really don't give a hoot about healthful greens, then forget the greens and look for berries. If you have this strange fetish about the mysteries of foods from under the earth, then dig arrowhead, Jerusalem artichokes, and gayfeather and forget everything else. You have this thing about cattail? Make cattail your specialty. I have friends who are interested only in morel mushrooms and wild asparagus, which means they have one or two weekends out of the year when they wander the ditches, woods, and fields gathering nature's treasures. For them, that's enough. And who's to say it isn't? Not me! If all you know how to identify is cattail, and you know only how to cook the young shoots . . . hey, you're going to know more than just about anyone else in your camp.

The Fat of the Land

It is a widespread misconception that Native tribes living by hunting and gathering must have struggled constantly with starvation. Not at all. The fact of the matter is, when a group of people lived on the same landscape for many generations, they came to know that land very well. And its plants. They knew exactly where the best places were to look for arrowhead roots or cattail pollen, precisely when wild plums were ready for picking, how to find elusive ground turnips . . . I am anything but an adept at this kind of thing. I have never had to live for any extended time entirely on what I could find growing on the land. And yet I know that if there is a problem, it's how to carry all the food that can be gathered in a few short minutes when I happen to be where wild food is ready for harvest.

Now, imagine living in a Pawnee village along the Loup River complex on the central Plains 400 years ago. All the women of your village knew all these things not simply by their own experience but by being privy to the knowledge of thousands of women like them over hundreds of generations. They knew every square inch of their hundreds of square miles of territory. They knew precisely what was edible, and when it should be picked, and where it was most easily found, and how to harvest it, and who to bring along to help with that harvest, and then how to prepare it for eating—or better yet preserve it for use later in the year when that particular food source was no longer available to them.

Not to mention the time of day to look for it. To be sure, a modern scientific botanist might argue with some historical

Native American ideas about plant foods. For example, Richard Fool Bull, a Lakota holy man, told me that it's best to sneak up on ripe chokecherries from downwind because if they sense you are coming after them, they turn bitter. And who's to argue with that? Especially me, since I suspect the same thing of morel mushrooms.

When I first got started with my interest in wild foods, I was particularly interested in learning about chicory. For many years I loved chicory coffee from New Orleans, and had paid premium prices for it. Hey, if this stuff was available for free in the wild, I wanted to know more about it. And then I started reading that chicory greens are also particularly good. And that the blue flower is so distinctive, the plant is easy to find and identify. That sounded like just my cup of tea. Or maybe cup of coffee.

In a conversation with a botanist at the small college where I was teaching at the time, the topic of chicory came up, and this friend told me that that very morning he had noticed that a huge patch of chicory in a wide shoulder between a highway and railroad right-of-way nearby. Wow, was I excited. He gave me exact directions to the location, and that very afternoon I jumped into my pickup truck and headed out with a shovel to dig me up some chicory roots! Imagine my disappointment, however, when I found nothing even faintly resembling what he had described as the stunning acre of brilliant blue flowers chicory sports, a color that has since become my favorite color in this world.

A couple of days later, I told him he must have had something wrong; I couldn't find a single chicory blossom to guide me to the patch. He was puzzled, because just that morning he had gone by the same place again and thought about me as he spotted the huge, stunning field of blue precisely where he had told me to look. Okay . . . that afternoon I set out again, this time with written directions. And I found . . . nothing. There were a few scruffy pinkish blossoms, but nothing even close to the grand display my friend had described.

Early the next morning I complained to him again that he had now twice sent me on a wild goose chase—or maybe wild chicory chase—and I no longer thought it was funny. Again, he was bewildered. "Let's go right now, and I'll show you," he said. He took me to the spot he had described, the place I had twice seen not a single chicory, and there it was . . . acres of stunning blue, hardly a square foot not blanketed with chicory. And then my friend remembered: Chicory blooms in the morning, fades to a pale pink, loses that day's petals, and after noon becomes a pedestrian green weed, no longer showing the most stunning blue in this world's spectrum!

You can hunt and find chicory during the afternoon, but your task will be a lot easier if you keep chicory hours and visit it in the morning.

But back to my point. Those who gathered foods for a village knew such things. Imagine for a moment the abundance that this provided. Not only could the people of a Pawnee village easily gather enough to feed the entire community for a week in a matter of a few hours, but they'd bring back enough to prepare and preserve for meals many moons in the future. Think about this: American Indians had (and

Chicory

Chicory is a lot like dandelions. For one thing, chicory has a gloriously beautiful flower. Secondly, the leaves and crowns are delicious, and the roots can be baked up to make an excellent coffee additive. In many parts of the world, even in this country increasingly, both dandelions and chicory are cultivated as farm crops. The recipes are the same as for dandelions. Chicory is often called "endive," and like the cultivated plant of that name, its leaves are an excellent salad green, simply washed and tossed. The crown of the plant—the blanched node between the leaves and root—is prized as a tender vegetable, steamed or boiled until tender, salted, and served.

My own attraction to chicory, aside from its beautiful blue flower, is in the first-year root. The second year of the plant's life, the single, slender taproot becomes multilegged and very woody and is not suitable for roasting for a drink. Normally I wouldn't go to all this trouble just to make a warm drink, but I am particularly fond of chicory coffee, a favorite I learned while in New Orleans. I don't think I would want to drink a brew made up of chicory alone, but as an addition to coffee, it's well worth my time. Dig and clean thoroughly the single taproots of the first-year plant. Place them on a cookie tray in an oven at about 250 degrees and roast until they are crisp and break with a snap. I like to keep mine roasting until they just begin to fume a bit. Be prepared for people to stop by your kitchen, because it will smell like you're baking chocolate chip cookies! When they're cool, snap and grind into pieces the size of a coarse-grind coffee and mix with coffee grounds to taste.

A little chicory goes a long way for me, but since I like strong coffee I mix about one part chicory to ten or twelve parts coffee. Then brew it up as you would any coffee. It will make the coffee a bit more bitter, a touch chocolaty. In New Orleans chicory coffee is often drunk *au lait,* with milk—that is, mixed almost half and half with warm milk, which neutralizes the coffee's acidity and the chicory's bitterness. You might just as well be drinking mocha! It's good!

to some extent still have) an incredibly rich repertoire of music, narrative, ritual, and oral history. It takes a lot of time to keep a complex cultural matrix like that up and going. After all, there was no writing, so everything had to be remembered. So where the heck did they find the time to do all these activities—to sing thousands of songs, observe day- and weeklong ceremonies, recite myths and historical accounts that took endless evenings—if they were constantly scrambling to find enough food to get them through the day?

You can't work from dawn to dark sorting grass grains from gravel and still have rich traditions like that. No, the actual fact is that there was plenty of time because there was plenty of food. Plains Indians didn't see the endless American steppes as a wasteland, devoid of life and cheer. Good grief, no! They saw what we see as emptiness as a bountiful garden land serving up more food than they could possibly harvest. Why, there wasn't enough time in the day to drag all the food back to the village! The bottom line is that they didn't try to "conquer" the West like the pioneers. They didn't have a "struggle" against the "cruelties" of nature. Nope, they sat back and sang prayers of gratitude for the incredible gifts of plenty that the Great Mysterious showered on them in this generous landscape. We can do the same—not only to eat well, rest easily, and have time for the important things of life like conversation, music, dance, love, ritual, and religion, but also to put ourselves again at peace with our Mother Earth. We need to remember what the Indians could have taught our pioneer forebears if they had had the sense to listen. Mother Earth is our friend, not our enemy. No conquering is necessary.

Let me be clear, however, that I am not suggesting that you live entirely by grazing ditches and parkways! Or even mostly by gathering. I have the occasional wild salad, I harvest whatever is in season that I really relish, and perhaps most of all, I take advantage of the occasional treat that presents itself as I head toward a fishing hole, walk the dogs down to the river, or take an afternoon stroll with my wife. We spot a bush laden with juicy, ripe mulberries, black or white, and so we stop and munch. It's like a gift from God. Mostly, I imagine, because it is. Linda and I once got stuck in some soft sand while on our way to a cemetery, and there along the road were dozens of sandcherry bushes, laden with fat, black berries. We ate our fill. A week earlier and they wouldn't have been ready; a week later and they would have been on the ground or in some raccoon's stomach. But we were there at precisely the right moment. Coincidence? I think not!

Even if you don't hunt (I don't) or fish (I do), you surely know nonetheless that your friends who do don't live by what they kill. Actually, in most cases what hunters and fishermen get in the field isn't really what's important. They'll tell you that. Maybe they don't even like venison or catfish. Well, it's the same way with weeds. Except that I do like the weeds I harvest. Thank the gods, I have never had to survive on wild plants. For me they are, as in the option I offer in my title, fun not fare. And yet what delicious fun they are.

Chapter Four

A PEELING STORY

 What is a weed? A plant whose virtues have not yet been discovered.

—Ralph Waldo Emerson

Which is not to diminish the very practical possibilities in knowing that there are wild foods all around you, as well as what they are and how to eat them! The chance that any of us will wind up in a situation where we have to survive on what we know about wild foods is, I suppose, slim. I'm sixty-nine years old, have done a lot of travel and wilderness living, and I've never been in that situation. But we do read now and again about people who wind up in a tough spot and have to scramble for something to eat.

Several times a year there is a news story about a plane wreck survivor, a lost hunter, a disaster victim in a remote part of the country, a traveler who has hit on some bad luck and needs to find food . . . and almost inevitably I wind up shaking my head at the reports and muttering something under my breath like, "Damn fool! He's no hero! *He's an idiot!*"

There was a classic case a few years ago. A hiker was somehow separated from his group, wandered astray, and became hopelessly lost in the wilderness. I think it was in Michigan somewhere. He survived for months by eating potato peelings from the garbage dump of a seasonal wood-cutters' camp he stumbled on. When he was found, he was on the edge of death, had lost half his weight, was little more than malnourished human wreckage. His family and community welcomed him as a returning hero. The media celebrated his tenacity and ingenuity. He was just pleased as hell with himself for surviving on rotting potato peelings.

But think about this. Indians prospered in that same area for millennia, never noticing any particular lack of vittles around them. Bears grow fat and lazy from the abundance of berries, fish, bugs, greens, frogs, cattails, roots, on and on and on and on. But this half-wit ate only moldy potato peelings from a garbage pit. Surrounded by a bounty, he chose instead to eat the very worst of what was available. Now, I can imagine being ignorant of what can be eaten, but not *that* ignorant! I can imagine being happy that Dad, or Hubby, or simply Alphonse from down the road has been found alive and will be returning home, but I sure as billy-hell can't imagine celebrating his genius for surviving on rotten potato peelings.

This whole thing about wild foods and weeds is in a way a reflection of my own goofy notions about life. I figure that what's important about life is not simply a matter of knowing but rather of learning. It's the process rather than the item. And I hope here to steer you in some directions where you can learn. There is no pat set of rules, directions, descriptions, lists, inventories, recipes, what have you, that I can give you to set you up to harvest and enjoy wild foods. There is no such thing, and any book that suggests it offers one is pure and simple hogwash. Whatever examples of wild foods I give you here are exactly that: examples. Not truth, but clues.

Getting to Know Use

So where *do* you go to find out the specifics of what you can find and enjoy by way of wild foods in your region of the world? Not everyone can spend decades hanging around an Indian reservation in the hope of finding a mentor to guide him or her down the roads of weeds. When I started my interest in wild foods, many decades ago, there were half a dozen books about the subject. I bought them all, and read them. They helped, but I still had to depend on human resources to show me specific plants, to talk to me about their uses, to give me recipes. We have come a long way since then. Now there are hundreds upon hundreds of books about wild foods, many dealing with relatively narrow geographic areas. An old friend, colleague, and one of the co-chairs of my political campaign for the Lancaster County Weed Authority, Kathleen Young, has since become a trained, educated, and experienced expert in Nebraska wild foods and medicines and has published her wonderful landmark book, *Wild Seasons: Gathering and Cooking Wild Plants of the Great*

A Cook's Apologia

When I wrote my book *Diggin' In and Piggin' Out* (HarperCollins, 1997), one of the jokes was to be that it would have one single recipe in it, my patented formula for "Gin and Tonic Ribs." Like most jokes, this one had a message: This is a book about eating, not cooking. I have been told—often by my wife, Linda—that I am not good at cooking. I am good at eating. In that book I listed every animal meat I could recall having eaten; I have since remembered others and added a few more to the list. On one occasion I came out of the kitchen with my supper plate on a make-your-own evening. Daughter Antonia looked at my plate—Bulgarian sheep cheese, Greek olives, a pre-packaged Pakistani dish, and some leftover barbecue ribs—and asked in all honesty and curiosity, "Dad, how do you decide what to eat?"

Excellent question. The answer is, I have no idea. I drift into the kitchen or our larder and let my mind dictate my appetites. That works well for me. Even when I cook, I can't tell you how I do whatever I do . . . some of this, some of that, whatever is left over, or within reach, maybe something of which there is only a little left, or maybe something I want to use up before it's more than three years past its use-before date, maybe something in the freezer than I can't identify but I've been curious about for the last couple of weeks . . .

They tell me that classical French recipe books don't provide quantities, just suggested ingredients. Your taste and experience determine how much you use of any one component in the dish. That really makes sense to me. You can't cook by formula, particularly if you are talking about wild foods that may be available in one place but not another, at one time but not another, in whatever quantities nature happens to provide at the time and place. And that's the way the cooking suggestions are going to be in the sidebars you'll find scattered along through these pages. Rather than being bound by modern American nonsense about one-sixty-fourth of a cup of something or another and trying to do something exactly the way everyone else does it, mix and cook "to taste." Have some fun. I don't know how big or sweet the Jerusalem artichokes are going to be where you read these pages, or what the crop will be like the year you read it, so it would be idle folly for me to try to tell you exactly how much cilantro to use to make your 14 ounces taste just right to you. So I won't even try. Dig around in your cupboard or fridge. Or backpack or tent. Look around the woods, fields, or backyard to see what else you can find to add to the mix. If it doesn't work . . . well, try again the next meal.

Plains. I had a hard time even finding a reliable and easily used guide for identifying plants on the Plains when I first became interested, but now there are again a dozen excellent, illustrated guides to Nebraska plants.

Obviously I cannot build a list for you of every book available to identify plants, edible or not, for every region of this nation. Some are obscure, limited-distribution books written for very small areas, after all. That task is yours. That's how you'll come to know your own region's plants—by getting to know what published resources there are for your region's plants. Visit libraries and bookstores, plow the Web, talk with local experts and weed nuts. Ask around. They are there. You'll find them.

Watch for classes and workshops offered by nature centers, park departments, community colleges, ag extension divisions, libraries, Boy Scout and Girl Scout offices, gardening nurseries . . . you get the idea. There are worlds of information out there and a world of ways to find it. If I have a regret in this long, rich, and varied life of mine, it's that the Web came along so late in it. What an incredible resource! Believe me, if you have questions about any specific plants, go to any search engine and plug in the name of that plant. If you have a problem at all, it is likely to be that you will come up with more information than you can quickly or conveniently sort through . . . almost surely including punk bands in Seattle named "Bastard Toad Flax" and "Pussy Field Toes."

Taming the Wilds

Shortly after I met Charles Kuralt and won my bid for a seat on the weed board, I had another big change in my life that bears on our discussion about weeds. I had a nice piece of land, about five acres, in the mountains behind Pikes Peak, near the town of Florissant, Colorado. It was within easy walk of a trout steam, nicely wooded (although I have heard that it has since been burned out), not a bad day's drive from my home in Lincoln. But then the price of gas went up, the speed limit on the interstate went down, and my marriage went sour. So I sold that ground and began to look for something closer to my home and closer to my heart. (I'm a Plainsman at heart, not a mountain man.) Totally by accident I was directed by an old friend to a piece of badly abused pastureland—nothing but sand, cacti, brush, and marshy river bottoms—in central Nebraska. I fell in love with it and the town near it instantly.

I saw this remote, rural site not only as a retreat from the city and the academic life but as something with a rationale a bit more sinister—a survival base. The time was the early 1970s. America was rocked with rioting, looting, ugliness from anarchists both in police uniform and bearing signs of political protest. Things didn't look at all good for this nation. As racial, social, and political riots sprang up even in small, bucolic cities like Lincoln and Omaha, Nebraska, it seemed possible to me that America was about to erupt and collapse in dramatic anarchy. It was a scary time. Not unlike the present day.

I am not a survivalist in the most common and very worst sense of that word—someone who hoards ammunition and supplies with the intent of persisting even at the cost of his fellow man. But neither did I want to see my family burned out and killed in the streets, which at that time seemed a very real and frightening possibility.

So I thought about what it would take to survive after a social apocalypse. I gathered lists from every source I could think of describing what might be necessary to bring a family through a time of enormous chaos and struggle. I sought out every survival list, plan, or plot, from the Boy Scouts to the Posse Comitatus. I checked out Civil Defense brochures, Red Cross lists, the military . . .

I found little comfort. How much junk can you carry, after all, on your back or in your car trunk? How much water can you store in your basement, and how much ammunition do you need to have stored up to kill your starving neighbors and preserve your Christian traditions? How long is long enough to stock up supplies for? A year? Two years? Ten years? If our society were razed to the ground, would things really be back on an even keel in a year? Ten years? How many barrels of water and boxes of hardtack crackers would you need to survive in your basement for, oh, fifteen years?

Once again I turned to thoughts about the history of my Indian friends. When a band of young men went out on the warpath, how much did they drag along by way of supplies? When an entire Omaha village went out on the winter buffalo hunt with no beasts of burden other than women and dogs, how much could they carry with them by way of food and supplies—especially considering that upon their return, they were (hopefully) going to be bringing back substantial loads of buffalo meat to get the village through the winter?

I really didn't have to guess. There is plenty of documentation for this information. Young men would set out on a trip from the Nebraska shores of the Missouri River to get flint from the Spanish Digs of what is now northeastern Wyoming, a trip of several months—or perhaps a shorter jaunt of a few weeks to get pipestone from the quarries in what is now southwestern Minnesota—with a couple of spare moccasins stuffed full of dried buffalo meat tied at their belt strings. And that was it. And to some degree that food stuffed in their moccasins was only a gesture of kindness from a well-wishing wife or family member and was taken only as an acknowledgment of the kindness. Thing is, the travelers actually didn't even need to take that.

The truth hit me like a blow from an oak two-by-four across my bean: What Indians needed for survival was not what they could carry on their backs but what they could carry in their brains. What would and could sustain them not just for days but for a lifetime was not what they owned but what they knew.

And yet, on the other hand, that shouldn't mean that a fellow shouldn't be prepared. So I did that, too. First, I learned all I could about edible wild foods, something anyone can do—and which after all you are already doing. But there's even more. You can, for example, get to know the land around you, or perhaps more precisely the land where you would probably wind up if you had to do some scrambling for survival. By that I mean no more than some hiking, hunting, fishing, picnicking . . . and keeping your eyes open for where the asparagus, milkweed, plums, and cattails are.

In my case there was no doubt where I would head if times got ugly. I had a sixty-acre parcel of wasteland on the banks of a clean, lovely river about 125 miles from my home.

I had looked at maps and checked out the route I would best travel if I needed to get out there on foot. (Forget your automobile if this kind of cataclysmic event should ever happen. It's nothing but a pain in the neck now, and it will be even more of a handicap when there is no gas and the roads are jammed with wreckage of other cars that idiots thought would carry them to some kind of temporary safety when *they* ran out of fuel.) And then I laid up supplies to feed on when and if I arrived in need of refuge.

Loading Up the Larder

Uh-huh, I know: I said that stockpiling is a waste of time. It is. I didn't pile up barrels of hard crackers, peanut butter, and water. Nope, I scouted out my land carefully and planted my vittles for the future where they would have the best chance to be happy and thrive and therefore help me be happy and survive should the need ever arise. My friend Richard Fool Bull had once pointed out that Indians didn't just stumble around hoping to find food. They knew where food grew naturally, but even more importantly, they made sure there was food where they might not have been any otherwise. It only makes sense. They weren't dummies. And if they prized arrowhead, wild turnips, gayfeather tubers, acorns, why would they just hope that Mother Nature took care of the planting and culturing? No, they planted and tended plots of "wild" foods, Fool Bull assured me. Mother Nature is fine but why not give her a hand when you can?

Now, think about it: I live a good 100 miles west of the natural distribution of oak trees. And yet about 200 yards from me is Oak Creek. And there are oak trees all along it. Natural distribution? Let's see, a squirrel somewhere along the Missouri River banks once carried an acorn 100 yards west and buried it. That acorn sprouted and grew a nice big oak tree. Fifty years later another squirrel took an acorn from that tree, carried it another 100 yards west, and buried it. A tree grew, an acorn fell, a squirrel toted . . .

Oh, come on! Don't be silly! Much more likely a scenario is that an Indian woman thought it would be nice to have some oak trees for fuel and food somewhere farther out west in the buffalo hunting grounds, somewhere along that nice creek that empties into Plenty Potatoes River. You know, where they always camped to dress hides and make jerky from the hunt. So she carried a small pouch of acorns with her on the next hunt and planted them eight or ten days out on the trip to the hunt. And they grew there and did just fine and her daughters and her daughters' daughters had fuel and food for the next couple of centuries. Until the white guys came along and cut down most of the trees and forgot how to eat the acorns. But I'm getting ahead of myself here. I have a lot more to say about acorns and Indian women—a *lot* more—later, in the chapter about nuts.

Back to storing up food for hard times. Indians didn't just store up food; they planned well enough in advance to set up a system for producing food over the long run. Well, you can do the same thing. Bring some gayfeather seeds along to your land, sprinkle them in a suitable place in a sandy soil clearing, scratch them into the soil a little, and for years you'll have the beauty of a flower favored by floral arrangers and flower shops—and food if you ever need it. Plant a few daylily roots down along a damp spot in the bottoms; they'll spread over the years until you have a glorious splash of orange every spring . . . and a storehouse of delicious food forever after. Plant walnut trees, and oaks like that Indian woman. Some Jerusalem artichokes in a fence corner, and wild grapes farther along the fence. Plant some hops under a fallen tree. It's a little bit like cheating—filling in the gaps where nature hasn't had the time to handle the job herself. Just a bit of a nudge in the right direction. Stored food goes stale and lasts only as long as the boxes and barrels are full; wild food is always there, always fresh.

A Shady Deal

There are other advantages to weeds that you might not think about. If you have a suburban, exurban, or even urban home, you are almost surely going to plant something—shrubbery, landscaping plants, a window box. You can plant almost anything, right? You probably want something that's pretty, maybe floral. Or perhaps you find yourself in a situation I was once in in my own suburban home. This was a walkout-basement, split-level, ranch-type brick house. The west side was therefore two stories of naked brick, exposed to the hot Nebraska sun for a good eight hours on the average July day. By the time evening rolled around, that wall was like a bake oven set on high broil. The patio below the wall was insufferably hot well into the next morning. If we opened the bedroom windows in that wall and over the patio, heat rolled in like the exhaust from a Finnish sauna.

Daylilies

Daylilies are like cattails: a veritable grocery store for the forager. Daylilies are not, strictly speaking, weeds, but it's not unusual to find patches of escaped domestic daylilies in woods, along roads, and scattered along riverbanks. There are several such plant communities within sight of where I sit writing this, in fact.

From root to flower, from bud to withered petals, the daylily will find a home on your kitchen table. Every day there are fresh buds on the common garden daylily—that's why they're called *day*lilies, after all. The buds are edible raw or cooked (boiled or steamed as a vegetable). Same with the roots. Dug, cleaned, and boiled they are a pleasing and nutritious vegetable. Some sources claim that the wilted flowers of the daylily are used in the Orient as a soup ingredient, as a thickener, but I can't speak to that claim. But hey, these are the people who make soup out of birds' nests, so anything is possible.

There was absolutely no room in the small space between the house and the garage—that is, the patio area—to plant a tree or shrubs to shade the patio or the wall. But we needed some shade there, and we needed it fast.

At the time I was doing some work and travel in Germany, and I thought of something that's fairly common there—a grape arbor. Especially along the Mosel and Rhine

Rivers where wine grapes are common and an economic asset, outdoor household, hotel, even restaurant areas had simple wire and light wood frames built over them, on which wine grapes grew. The vines grow very fast: half a foot to a foot a day in the spring. The broad and abundant leaves provide generous shade. Heat easily passes up through the leaves and vines. In the winter, when the sun provides welcome warmth, the leaves are gone and the sun shines through. The arbors are not burdened by heavy loads of snow, because it falls through the vines. And of course in the autumn, you have a wonderful harvest of grapes.

Hmmm, I thought . . . I wonder if that will work for the west wall of my home? I planted a couple of cuttings from wild grapes I had found along the river in wooden half barrels on our patio. I staked a couple of strands of heavy wire to the ground and ran them to the eaves of the house two stories above. And in a matter of a month, I had two stories of shade. The change was astonishing: The house was cooler, but not shaded in the winter when we welcomed the sun against the west wall. Our patio was actually usable again. And there were some unexpected side benefits: A robin built a nest in the vines immediately outside our bedroom window where we could keep track of the eggs and, eventually, the babies. In the fall we had a bounty of wild grapes for wine, right in our backyard rather than in a distant woods on someone else's land.

There were grapes on one of the vines, at least. As I later found out, wild American labrusca grapes are different from European vinifera grapes in that they are sexed—that is, there are male and female plants. Fortunately, I had by chance wound up with one of each for my home arbor. If you don't want to be tracking grape stains onto your white carpet, therefore, take your cuttings from a wild vine that has no grapes on it in the autumn; on the other hand, if you want the grapes, find yourself a female vine.

Or even if you don't want the grapes, there may be others who do. When I established a new home with another tall west wall out in the country, I once again planted wild grapes for shade and cover. Once again I've enjoyed birds' nests for easy viewing. And since I planted female vines, I've found that all winter long I have cardinals at my bedroom window enjoying a breakfast of raisined grapes, while in the spring, the first thing newly arrived robins do is take advantage of easily picked high-energy raisins still hanging dried on my grapevines.

I recently heard a vigorous rustling outside my bedroom window early in the morning and looked out to see if it was a bunch of robins being particularly energetic at the harvest. I was amazed to see my two big ol' black Lab dogs standing at the base of the vines, pulling grapes within their reach from the vines with their mouths, munching away, their mouths and tongues glowingly purple. They know a good thing when they taste it! See? You never know who is going to wind up enjoying your wild grapes!

Even if your grapes are nowhere near your entryway or a patio, birds have a way, if you catch my drift, of, uh, carrying grapes and mulberries to roosts immediately above your car, especially if it is newly washed, and depositing the deep purple stains on the windshield. If you want the shade but not the mess that can come with grape stains, there are other wild plants you can use for shade and enjoyment. I am partial to hops, for example. A lot of Germans settled in Nebraska, and a lot of them grew their hops to make their own beer. Hops do well in the wild, and so it's really not unusual around here to run into the occasional patch of wild hops climbing up a windmill tower or over a pasture fence. I got some hops plantings from a fence near Lincoln and some others from along the banks of the Niobrara River while I was on a canoeing trip one spring. They come up every year and thrive. I use them to shade the walls of my summer kitchen and the south side of my shop. In the fall I harvest a mess of the cones for sachets and teas, and I always have plenty to give to friends and family as Christmas presents.

Great Escapes

I have planted some wild onions under the drain drips of my study's air conditioner, where they get a bit more water than this parched Plains ground might otherwise expect. They thrive and I enjoy them, grabbing a few stems every now and then to freshen my breath before I go to the town tavern and repel all the locals, lighting cigars and peeling paint with my exhales.

In fact, a lot of "wild" foods are actually escaped "domestics," plants that are not at all native but have somehow found their way into a wild setting. My land sits along a Plains river, and I am constantly surprised to find patches of iris and lily of the valley, clearly not native plants but something that has probably washed down during a flood from well upstream, a bulb or two flushed out of a pioneer garden perhaps and then lodged here on the banks of my own place where they now thrive decades later. Wild asparagus is actually an escaped domestic, as are my wild onions. Now, these plants have in some cases become feral—regressed, if it is indeed regression—to an earlier, wilder form . . . perhaps smaller, like wild strawberries, and probably stronger, like wild onions. Frankly, I think that makes them all the better: You don't have to pick as many to get the same if not richer flavor.

In other cases the wild varieties are the original forms of the plants from which the domesticated plants in field and garden were bred. I think that's the case with my wild onions. They are much smaller and potent in taste than anything I have ever tasted along the line of domestic onions. It doesn't take much of these pungent puppies to go a long way. Nonetheless, when I know Linda is going to be gone long enough for the power to fade, I tug up a couple of these flavor bombs, wash them off, and eat them right there in the backyard. Terrific!

Turnabout Is Fare Play

It's not just a matter of plants moving from domestication back into the wild, either. The passage from one category to another is constant and moves in both ways. There are still some damn clever folks out there listening and learning about how wild plants can be turned to man's use and be tamed, which is to say planted and cultivated. Who know what they will come up with next, but every year it seems I read about someone trying an alternative crop of one weed or another. Chicory, for example, is now being grown on the Plains as a sugar source. I would love to see *that* field in bloom!

Perhaps the wackiest and therefore most interesting use of wild plants I have encountered in the last couple of decades came from the unlikely genius of a former student of mine, Herb Knudsen of Ogallala, Nebraska. He is creating an industry out of milkweed. Plain ol' milkweed. He harvests the mature pods for their silky, soft, puffy "down" and incorporates it into all manner of applications where avian down, or other insulating, bulk fibers might be used: comforters, winter clothing, robes, that kind of thing. Farmers in the area have turned from the madness of a maize monoculture that is increasingly less productive and are growing the very weed they have fought for so many years between the cornrows—milkweed. Reports suggest that the stuff grows like . . . well, like weeds.

Chapter Five

WHOSE LAND IS IT, ANYWAY?

 **. . . Wet and wilderness? Let them be left.
O let them be left, wilderness and wet.
Long live the weeds and the wildness!**
—Gerard Manley Hopkins

The reality of gathering wild foods can be even more spiritually meaningful than man's respect for nature. In some cases, the gift of food for us is a device of survival for the *plants*. A patch of arrowhead may do just fine, even prosper, while never being visited by a human being. After all, there aren't very many people out there digging up arrowhead bulbs for their table from the stinking muck of a slough!

I was once doing exactly that in a backwater marsh of a state lake near my home of Lincoln, Nebraska. The lake's water level was down, leaving the marsh and its dense population of arrowhead more accessible than usual. But not really all *that* accessible. I waded through the smelly, black muck out to the bed with a short shovel and was sorting through the slime to find the toe-size (and -shaped) tubers for my bucket. I suppose I had accumulated a couple of gallons of the tubers, which was about my limit, since they are not easily stored for any length of time after harvesting and need to be cooked and eaten pretty much in the next couple of days after gathering. I was covered with stinking muck, and the prizes in my bucket looked and smelled for all the world like something I should be tossing in the trash.

I thought about the wisdom of Indian women when they gathered the same tubers: They preferred to stand in waist- or knee-deep water, feeling for the bulbs with their toes, freeing them from the mother plant and muck, and then picking them up as they floated to the top of the water. Definitely a superior and cleaner way of doing things than what I was doing that day.

About the time that I was ready to wade back across the swamp to the shore and to my car (how was I going to keep this filthy mess from the fenders, not to mention the seats?), a state truck came rolling up. I could see by the uniform and officious manner of the driver that I was probably in for some trouble here. No, I had a park permit, so I was okay there. Maybe I was violating some rule by parking along the road? Well, here comes Smokey, so I'll find out soon enough what his complaint is.

He wanted to know what I was doing. I told him I was digging arrowhead roots. He peered dubiously into my bucket of muck and lumps. He wanted to know what I was going to do with them. I told him I was going to take them home and eat them. He became even more dubious. But then he waxed philosophical . . . and I had him right where I wanted him. "What would happen if everyone came here and dug up those . . . what did you call them? Arrowhead? . . . Arrowhead roots?"

Well, I'd thought I had him where I wanted him, but frankly his conundrum had me stumped. Wow. I had never thought of that, because in all my years I had never encountered a single other human being harvesting arrowhead. Not one. Not anywhere. The thought of *everyone* gathering arrowhead right here in this Nebraska backwater simply stopped me in my theoretical steps. Wow . . . "What if everyone were gathering arrowhead . . ."

Even before he could interrupt to call me a smart-ass, I did some further thinking aloud: "I suppose if everyone who came out here dug up arrowhead roots . . . all of Lancaster County would be overgrown by arrowhead." Arrowhead propagates, after all, when its tubers are washed out by flooding waters, or eroding banks, or by being dug up by raccoons, beaver, and weed eaters, inevitably freeing some tubers to float away and start a new bed elsewhere. The fact of the matter is, I told this Guardian of Nature, when arrowhead is harvested, it is simultaneously spread, encouraged, and renewed. Far from damaging this bed of marsh plants under his official protection, I was cultivating it even as I was harvesting it.

He looked at me in disbelief. Now I had stumped him. He was now in the position of interrupting someone in the process of improving the property he was supposed to be protecting. You could almost hear the gears in his head turning and grinding while he was contemplating this blasphemous line of thinking.

"Well . . . don't let me catch you digging up arrowhead roots here again," he said, watching me with continued suspicion as I put my bucket of filthy stuff in the trunk, spread a tarp on my car seat, and drove off. I took his admonition to heart, too. I never did let him catch me again.

This Land Is *Not* Your Land

And yet . . . the whole incident got me thinking. Woody Guthrie notwithstanding—by what right do we harvest the fruits of the earth? Whose land *is* this, anyway?

I recently had some trouble with a neighbor. Actually, not a neighbor but a half-wit who lives a couple of plots of ground up the river. He blithely helped himself to my river bottom, putting up a duck blind on my land, cutting himself a generous path through my undergrowth, spraying and killing a large patch of staghorn sumac I loved and harvested annually, herding his horses around the ends of my fences and through my property lines . . . (This idiot said he was spraying *poison* sumac. There is no poison sumac in this region, only *staghorn* sumac, a totally different—and edible—plant. Which is to say, this guy was acting as so many do out of utter ignorance.)

When confronted with the offensiveness of his trespassing, he offered up a variety of explanations. First he said, well, uh, river bottom is everyone's property. That, sadly, seems to be a widespread misunderstanding of property law. People who buy "all-terrain" vehicles seem to live

Sumac

Staghorn sumac is called "staghorn" because its jagged, thick, velvet-covered branches look for all the world like stags' horns. I like this plant a lot. It's nice enough as wildlife cover, but in autumn it turns a spectacular red that blazes like fire all across the Plains landscape. It has large clusters of red, velvety berries after midsummer and well into the fall. The berries aren't exactly edible, but they make a delightful drink that looks for all the world like pink lemonade. The way to use the berries is easy enough: Pick some, blow the dust off them, and drop them into a cup of cold water. Strain out the berries after a bit, and you have pink lemonade. On hikes down to the river here on my own place, I grab a few berries as I pass my sumac groves and pop them into my mouth, suck on them a moment, and spit them out. The result is a really nice, tangy, refreshing blast of lemony flavor.

under the goofy notion that that phrase actually means *all terrain*. No, my land is still *my* land. And you are not welcome on it with your noise, smell, and destructive ways, *all-terrain* plaything or not. In fact, if you have enough money to blow on such an expensive toy, why is it you don't also have the resources to buy the terrain to drive it on? You ask that question and they stare at you blankly, perhaps complaining that taxes are too high. Idiots!

My distant neighbor, once disabused of the notion that my land is public domain, explained that then, uh, well, since river bottoms are useless ground, he figured I wouldn't make such a fuss about him helping himself to it. I then offered that instead of him caretaking my useless river bottoms, how about I take possession of *his* useless river-bottom property instead? He didn't think that was a very good idea at all, as it turns out.

In my state and most others, there is no ownerless land. There is state-owned land where you may or may not be able to explore freely, but in Nebraska even a lot of game and parkland requires the purchase of a permit for visiting. In fact, in the case of my own property, I own the ground under the river to midstream—not the water, but the land under it. So canoers floating past are on state water as they float by, but the minute they snag up on a sandbar and get out to drag their craft back into the channel, they are on my land.

Now, I'm not fussy about canoers, fishermen, or a lot of other things. Families picnicking, kids swimming along or even on my property—all that is fine with me. But shooters, motor vehicles, drunks, fireworks, and certainly "all-terrain" vehicles ripping up the riverbed, wet or dry, are trespassing, plain and simple. That is not welcome and I have the right to forbid that kind of activity on my land. And I do.

The point of this is, before you hunt mushrooms or asparagus on land—even if it seems to be useless, unoccupied, public wasteland—it is as important to ask permission of the owner as it is to ask permission for hunting deer or pheasant on the same ground. Most landowners look favorably on the quiet, careful, courteous plant hunter, even when, as so often happens these days, the owners have not had happy experiences with game hunters. But still, you need to ask permission before helping yourself to land someone else pays the taxes on. Besides, it's the nice thing to do. And the safe thing to do. You need to know if the owner is going to be plinking with his AK-47 down in that direction in the next half hour or so, or if there is a mountain lion living in the woods below the house (which is the case with our place these days!), or if the nuclear waste dump behind the barn has been leaking steaming glow-in-the-dark vapors over the last couple of months.

In Fact, This Land Isn't Even *My* Land

Know what? I feel the same sense of responsibility even when I'm foraging on my own land. Because it's not really mine, either. I am only borrowing it for the short span of my lifetime. I suppose if ownership comes down to prior occupation or tenure, it is Pawnee ground. Or buffalo ground. The considerable Native American influences in my life tell me that the land doesn't even belong to them, however, but to the Great Mysterious, that unknown and unknowable power that moves and motivates everything around us. Nowhere are those mysteries more obvious, after all, than precisely where you and I are going to be gathering our plants, nor more evident than in the bounty of those plants themselves.

Plains Indians always accepted the gratitude of the bison after a kill even as they thanked the bison. They figured that just as it was their role in the grander scheme of things to kill buffalo, it was the buffalo's role—even pleasure—to play its role of providing food, clothing, shelter, and spiritual uplift for the people with whom it was inextricably bound in this grand circle of life. I feel that way. Whatever your philosophy of food, the fact remains that the only way we can live is if something dies. Does a cattail really have any less will to live than a buffalo does? Or than we ourselves do? I doubt it. They may not scream as loudly as they die, but die they do.

The secret, in my mind and in the minds of those who occupied and prospered from this landscape for so long before now, is a prevailing understanding of gratitude and respect for the sacrifices that other beings, from cattails to bison, make for us to continue living. I like that way of looking at things, and I try to live by it. My adopted Omaha brother Buddy Gilpin perhaps taught me best when he expressed his surprise at the white man's desire to have a moment of prayer at school, or before a meal, or one day a week, or one day a year. His words stunned me with their obvious and powerful wisdom: "Shouldn't each moment of our lives be a prayer of gratitude?" Yes, Buddy, each moment of our lives *should* be a prayer of gratitude.

Nor should our approach simply be an attitude but a genuine *effort* of respect. When gathering wild foods, we should never be wasteful, the ultimate act of disrespect. Never take more than you need or can use. Never strip a plant, patch, or vine. Pick carefully so as not to damage the mother plant. After all, that is a practical consideration, since you may hope to return again to this same plant, patch, or vine the next harvest season.

Chapter Six

THE MOREL OF
THE STORY

Each humblest plant, or weed, as we call it, stands there to express some thought or mood of ours.

—Henry David Thoreau

I think mushrooms are the most interesting wild food for a number of reasons—mostly contradictory. But then I find that the contradictions in life far more interesting than the consistencies. Mushrooms are probably the most supreme delicacy in the world of wild food—and if you don't believe me, check out the price of French black truffles somewhere on the Web or in a gourmet catalog. Or for that matter, go to your local upscale grocery store toward the end of next April and see what morel mushrooms are going for. Many mushrooms sell by the ounce—like caviar.

But obviously wild food gatherers aren't really out there wading through the woods, getting scratched up, picking up dozens of ticks and maybe poison ivy to save a few dollars at supper. There has to be more to it than a matter of economy. It's not at all unusual for people to drive hours to a favorite 'shrooming site to see how the morels are coming along.

The secrecy surrounding those sites is the stuff of spy novels. No kidding, I know people who leave early in the morning, before dawn, having told no one where they're going, taking nothing to the car that would suggest anything but perhaps a picnic or a trip to an amusement park. On departure they drive in a random direction and circle back in several loops to be sure they are not being followed by someone who wants to know where they are getting those huge, beautiful morels. On arrival at their secret location, they conceal their car or truck in the brush. I have heard rumor of uninvited followers being shot at . . . accidentally, of course.

While searching, the rabid "'shroomers," as they are called, employ personal tricks to ensure or at least encourage their success. I make a point upon spotting my first morel of the season to walk all around it, looking at it from every direction, tuning my eyes to the morel's unique texture and color. I get down on my knees and look at it again, from all directions. Then, and only then, do I bring out a bag in which I will gather my morels, because morels will hide if they see you coming with a big sack to collect them. Or something like that. I'm pretty sure. Whenever I find a morel, I instantly turn and go back along the path from which I came because it is almost certain that I have just walked past ten I didn't see, but now that my eyes are tuned—or maybe because I have given appropriate respect to the Morel God—I suddenly see them where moments before I saw nothing.

A good friend of mine has a secret for spotting morels that is absolutely uncanny. The day he decided to share his secret with me was like an act of brotherhood . . . I couldn't believe he was doing it. And then, when he showed me The Golden Key, I couldn't believe that there it was, right in front of me all along. Some other close, good friend had once shared this incredible, simple secret of spotting mushrooms with him, and now here he was sharing it with me. That secret is so simple, it's like fishing with dynamite. Will I share that secret with you? No.

No one goes through maneuvers like this to save a couple of bucks at the grocery store. There is just something about mushrooms. In the case of morels, and in the case of me, it's a matter of timing. Morels are variously timed as appearing the last weekend in April, or when the lilacs bloom (but be careful: I know for a fact that the lilacs and morels are one week later, at least, here than they are only 120 miles to the east), or when the lilies of the valley are in full growth but not yet blooming, and when the slower wild plum blossoms are still perfuming the air but are being overtaken by the heavy, sweet smell of the chokecherries. Or maybe morel mushrooms are like sweet corn . . . ready to be picked about two days after the raccoons clean out the garden. That is to say, morels are ready for the picking in midspring, just when I want to be out enjoying nature.

I think there is also something attractive to us about the mystery of mushrooms. We see the plum and chokecherry bushes bloom, so we know there will soon be fruit there. And we see last year's asparagus feathers blowing in the wind all year long and we know that the next year there will be those tender spears once again right at the base of those feathery fronds (and about the same time as the morels, by the way). But morels seem to spring from nowhere. We can't be at all sure that we will find them again this year where we found them last year. In fact, it seems that they make a point of *not* appearing where they did last year. There are no pre-emergence signs of morel mushrooms at all. One day there is nothing . . . and the next day, there they are. They don't actually "grow" at all; they magically appear like little tan ghosts on the forest floor.

Until recently even scientists didn't know how morel mushrooms grow—what sort of soils they like, what they feed on. Now they have the science down, and you can even buy kits that let you propagate morels on your own property. It's not simple, but you can do it. (By the way, there are also kits for growing button mushrooms, shiitakes, and more, under your laundry room sink. If I think of it before I finish talking with you here, I'll look up some addresses. Growing mushrooms is a lot of fun and probably safer, but not as much fun as going out into the woods to find wild ones.)

Like diamonds, the best mushrooms are rare. They are not easy to find, they are not easy to gather, they appear one day and a day or two later they are again gone for the year. Either you are there, or you are not. And yet they are every-where. I mean, jeez, fungus grows in our ears and between our toes! Small wonder we find it in urban alleys, big river valleys, remote foothills canyons . . . everywhere.

Mushrooms are not just edible; they are delicacies. They

are a gourmet treat of extraordinary appeal to even the finest palate. On the other hand, they are so deadly poisonous and bring on such grim forms of death that they should be gathered and eaten only with the utmost care and understanding.

The metaphor I usually use is that of the Borneo tribesman going shopping in a Kmart grocery section. He wouldn't know where to start. He'd sample the Drano, maybe chew on a cracker box. He'd eat the orange, peel and all, figure a can of sardines was inedible altogether. That's how the uninformed person in the woods and fields looks for food, too. You have to *know* what is edible and what is not. Poke shoots are a delicacy; the adult stems, root, and berries are poison. You have to know that. Okay, maybe you don't have to know that . . . if death means nothing to you. But you get the idea: You can't count on mushrooms being okay because they taste good; the death angel mushroom tastes very good, samplers have reported just before they started the long, painful process of dying.

There is a half-wit here in our area who tastes mushrooms to see if they are edible. I'm not sure if he tastes them because he is a half-wit or is a half-wit because he has tasted them. And for Pete's sake, don't listen to anyone who tells you that poisonous mushrooms turn sterling silver black, or who tells you that toadstools are poisonous while mushrooms are not. All that is pure flapdoodle. You have to *know* what you're doing. There is no guessing or hoping when it comes to mushroom, only staying alive or dying.

And that is easy enough. Get a good book with clear illustrations, study it, and then, most importantly, find someone friendly enough to go with you or take you along out into the field and show you what a morel looks like. Once you see one, you will never go astray. Morels are that distinctive. Once when my wife, Linda, was driving my mother somewhere or another and a wild turkey strutted across the road in front of them. Linda stopped and told Mom to look at the turkey. "How can you tell that's a turkey and not a pheasant?" Mom asked, not exactly being an outdoors-woman.

"How do we know it's a turkey and not a cow?" Linda sputtered.

You'll be that way about morels once you've seen one. You won't mistake a morel mushroom for a turkey *or* a cow.

I start with morel mushrooms because they are the very best, not just to my taste but to the preference of a lot of other folks, too. They are easily identified and therefore among the safest wild mushrooms. And they offer a wide range for preparation . . . in the unlikely event that you have any left after cleaning your find, rolling them in flour, frying them in butter, and then gorging yourself on them until you don't care if you ever eat another mushroom the rest of your life.

Morels are sometimes called "coral mushrooms" because they look a little like coral: pitted with depressions, a pale brown, about the size of your thumb. (More about that statement below, however!) There are false morels that may be toxic; the verdict isn't in. Morels are found—just about anywhere. Mushroomers have tried for generations to figure out what combination is the key to morel propagation— elm trees? Hackberries? I know for a fact that they don't seem to like maples. Oh . . . you think they *do* like maples . . .

Morels a la Bob

When I can't get down into my river bottoms to look for mushrooms, I give permission to my friend Bob Kawamoto to do his hunting down there—partially because he's a friend, partially because he generously drops off a bag of his find here in our kitchen before leaving. When I eat morels, I just drop them into soup, gravy, stew, or roast and eat them as is. Sometimes I toss some into a frying pan with a little butter and salt. Bob is a little fancier in his preparation of morels, and so I have asked him to share his secrets with us for these pages.

As with all good recipes the preparation of morels begins in the dead of winter. Sit by a fire with a good glass of scotch and begin the process of anticipation. Dream about the pungent smell, the earthy taste, the warm spring day when you will comb the woods. Anticipate the smile that will surely cross your face when you first bite that tiny morsel, hot, fresh, and full of flavor. A flavor of woods. A flavor that comes only once a year. A flavor that comes only after a long winter.

The second step of the recipe is the day. That perfect day. That long-awaited day, when the lilac has just started to bloom. The red oak's leaves are only as big as a squirrel's ear. The rain has come about every other day. And on the days it isn't raining, it's about seventy degrees Fahren-

heit. That perfect spring day when the morels pop from the ground.

Now, are you worthy of finding morels? That's the third part of the recipe. Have you thought about it long enough? Have you thought about it hard enough? Have you anticipated it enough so that your first half hour in the woods your eyes focus on everything and nothing at the same time? Do you dream about morels? Perhaps you are ready. Have you got the perfect patch of woods? Do you have the right equipment? All you need is a pocketknife and a small bag. The best knife would be one that belonged to your father. Better still, one that was made by your father. The bag should be made of mesh. The spores of the morel can fall out that way and replenish the woods.

Okay, finally, you find morels. All of the forces of nature and luck have smiled on you and your bag is full. Now what? Take them home and place them in a bucket of salted water. This will help kill or flush the hundreds of tiny residents that find homes in the dimples of the morel. The morel looks like a sponge and therefore makes lots of tiny homes for lots of tiny creatures. They're all fairly edible. However, some people prefer pure morels to protein-enhanced morels. Soak them for a half hour or so and then cut them in half, lengthwise. Plunge them in and out of clean water to help flush out sand, grit, bugs, leaves, dirt, and the occasional spider. Pat the halves dry on a paper towel.

I know a rather sophisticated fellow who insists that I bring him a bag of morels when the opportunity comes about. He takes the precious fungi and dices them, putting them into a rich butter- and cream-based sauce with thyme and rosemary, poured over penne pasta mixed with steamed vegetables and served with a chardonnay. He should be shot. He has tried to raise the bar on perfection. Simple. He missed simple.

After you have drained the morels on a paper towel, have two bowls ready. One will contain a mixture of an egg with a half cup of milk. The other, a mixture of two cups bread crumbs (plain, not seasoned), black pepper (about a half teaspoon to taste), a few dashes of salt, and about a half cup of crushed Ritz cracker crumbs. Run the morel halves through the egg-milk mixture, dredge through the crumb mixture, and then plunge into cast-iron frying pan that has a mixture covering the bottom of about a quarter inch of butter and vegetable oil. Cast iron is better. It's harder to learn to control the heat. But cast iron is better. Things taste better. I've never held my Teflon in much esteem. But my grandmother's cast iron is priceless. I prefer not to use olive oil because in my opinion the taste detracts from the butter and I use the vegetable oil because it allows the butter to rise to a higher temperature before it turns brown. You really don't want it to turn brown. Once the mushroom is in the butter and oil, allow it to cook to a golden color on both sides. After removing from the oil, place on a paper towel to drain.

Here is the trickiest part of the recipe. Knowing when to eat. Do not wait for fifteen minutes to pass. The mushroom, which gives off a lot of moisture when frying, will get a little limp as time passes. If you wait, you will have limp, only warm, mushrooms. It's better if you have a nice glass of red wine (I would suggest a nice merlot, or cabernet) already poured and waiting. As the mushroom hits the paper towel, rests for about thirty seconds to one minute, eat it. The first one should create that silly smile on your face that I mentioned earlier. Sip a little wine. Eat another. And so forth. Here's a trick just in case you mess up and don't eat quick enough. Place the plate with the mushrooms in an oven at about 300 degrees Fahrenheit for about ten minutes. They'll crisp up a little. Don't leave them too long or you'll have morel crackers. Not bad. But not what you dreamed about.

Now, I'd tell you how to dry mushrooms, freeze mushrooms, or in some other manner preserve them for later. If you have so many mushrooms that you can't eat them all at one time and are considering saving them, you must not have friends. I don't recall ever having any left over.

> *Lucky that way, I guess. There are morels avail-able now in certain gourmet stores and on the Internet. Commercial morels. I can't recommend them. I'm not sure whose manure they were raised in. I can't vouch for how they were cleaned. I can't say that whoever gathered them cared. I can only speak for those in my own bucket. So I eat until I am stuffed. Satiated in butter and mushrooms and tastes that come once a year. On that perfect day. After a long win-ter. If I am worthy.*
>
> I forgot to mention . . . Bob is also a pretty good writer.

never mind. On the high bank? Down in the depressions? Shade? Sun? I've been at this for a long time and I still don't have a clue.

Mushroom Clouds

I once traveled 30 miles, unloaded a canoe, dragged it to the water's edge, and paddled out to an island in the Platte River to a favorite morel hunting spot of mine. I found maybe ten small morels. What a disappointment. What did I do to offend the mushroom gods? I wondered. I drove home, defeated. All that way, all that trouble for nothing. I noticed that the garbage in the kitchen smelled a bit wangy. (I was a bachelor at the time, so chances are the place smelled to high heaven, actually.) I pulled the garbage bag out of the container and headed out to the alley. And . . . well, you can imagine what I found on the short walk across my backyard. Yep, dozens of morels, right there in my backyard where I had never before seen a single mushroom.

I think morels have a personality. I think they do this kind of thing on purpose. They do it to rub your nose in the fact that whatever you may think, *they* are ultimately in charge of what you will get, and when. When it comes to morels, smart-asses never win. On another occasion I was on the Platte River in a canoe with a student who was studying edible wild plants. We were part of a larger group of students with their teacher, so while I was offering up information to the larger crowd, my immediate task was to teach this young woman what I knew about what we saw, or about what we were looking for.

It was late April so we almost immediately found some asparagus and ate it on the spot, the way I like it—raw. She was delighted, but she wanted to know more about morels. On an island while stopped for lunch, we stumbled into a large patch of aromatic spearmint, so we picked a mess of it for tea. Another triumph—but, uh, what about morels? I said that we would almost certainly find morels at this time of the year, but that they are elusive and unpredictable, so . . . who knows? In the canoe, drifting along the bank, watching the passing herbage, I told her what to look for: smallish, light brown crowns, about the size of your thumb, pocked with depressions, looking like coral.

"Is that a morel then up there?" she said, pointing onto a small island we were floating past. Uh, well . . . gulp . . . yes, but . . . Almost in a panic I grabbed a passing branch and pulled our canoe to the bank. "Are you okay?" she asked me, sensing that I had almost wet my pants and was breathing only with difficulty. I should have known—having described morels to the best of my ability, establishing in the young mind of the woman with me what the typical morel was going to look like and what she should be looking for, the Morel Gods once again made the expert into the fool.

I sat there, gasping, hardly able to speak. The morel she was pointing to was literally the size of my head. I had never before seen a morel a twentieth that size, and yet there it was, perfect. We got out of the canoe and approached this giant. And over there, by that tree, there was another, just as big. And another and another. We returned to the canoe with a dozen mushrooms—not much of a find normally, but in this case more than we could easily carry in both our arms. And what's more, they were double mushrooms, one inside the other, so that each mushroom was actually two! That evening we sliced each morel in half, making four halves, and covered large steaks cooked over the campfire each with *one* quarter of *one* morel! I have since seen two morels almost that size, but these were my first. And think of the damage done to all the young minds we were dealing with in that camp that night: About twenty students went home from that trip with no possible other understanding than that morels (1) are as big as a football; (2) are cut into four halves because there is another mushroom inside; and (3) can scarcely be hard to find since they stand out like me in a beauty contest.

Experiences like this—and believe me, there are more!—

have given me enormous respect for morels. I try to treat them with care and appreciation when I'm picking them, and I think it pays off. I never pull them up by their "roots"; mushrooms are actually the "fruit" of an organism that lies under the soil or within the wood, and I am uneasy about damaging the fabric of that organism by tearing the mushrooms from the ground. (I break them off carefully or cut them.) Even if you don't embrace this notion of prescient mushrooms, it's still a good idea to be careful when gathering morels—they're hard enough to clean as it is without tossing dirt and sand into the sack along with them. All those depressions in morels turn into dirt magnets once they're in your gathering bag.

Fungus among Us

There are other mushrooms that are easily identified (and therefore relatively safe), easily found, easily prepared, and the stuff of the epicure's table. I like inky caps, their close cousins the shaggymanes (both of the *Coprinus* genus), puffballs, and bracket fungi for exactly the above reasons. I don't think mushrooms are worth taking a chance for, so I play it safe, and I don't want to hang by my toes from a mountain crag to get them or go through a lot of fuss to prepare them. So this short inventory is pretty much what I restrict my 'shrooming to.

Inky caps are exceedingly common mushrooms, and delicious. What's more, they can pop up just about any time of the year, certainly in the spring and again in the autumn depending on moisture. (Morels are available only in the

Morels

When I bring my morels back to the house, I rinse them thoroughly to get off what dirt and sand I can easily remove. Then I split them lengthwise and rinse them again since there are often small mites and mealybugs inside them. Then I soak them in lightly salted water to further clean out whatever buggy visitors may have hidden in their craggy recesses. My notions of preparing things to eat are typically male—I don't do much but eat. (I have discussed in detail my feelings about food in the book *Diggin' In and Piggin' Out: One Man's Love for Real Food, Home Cookin' and High Spirits.*) I sometimes roll morels in flour and then toss them into a pan with butter. And that's it. Morels are terrific with any meat, but as far as I'm concerned, they don't need anything more than themselves to be fully appreciated.

A real advantage to morels not shared by a lot of other mushrooms is that they lend themselves well to drying and freezing. The processes are again as simple as can be: Spread them some place clean and dry and let them dry, or throw them into a plastic bag and toss them into the freezer. There may be fancier ways, but I don't trouble with them in my kitchen.

spring.) Again, I recommend that you consult a good guide with illustrations to start you toward identification, and then ask someone who knows mushrooms to show you the real thing. Inky caps are smallish brown mushrooms that grow in clusters. They love old elm stumps, which means you can find them all across America, and pretty much at any time of the year—as opposed to morels, which have a very short period of availability. Inky caps are so called because as they age, they dissolve into a puddle of black goo. In fact, inky caps "autodigest." That is . . . gulp . . . *they eat themselves!* How's that for material for a science fiction novel?

A close relative with a similar habit of ending life on this earth in a black gooey mess is the shaggymane, thus called because its tall, white cap is fringed with shaggy shreds when fully grown.

A word of caution when it comes to these two: Some people find they have trouble when they ingest inky caps or shaggymanes with alcohol—stomach discomfort or even mental fuzziness. Of course, if you drink two bottles of wine while eating a couple of tablespoons of inky caps, what do you expect? Seriously, I avoid mixing alcohol with these two mushrooms. No sense in taking chances. And do know that some people are more sensitive to this than others. Mainly I want you to know that if you should mix the two and get queasy or blurry, you haven't poisoned yourself. Or your guests.

Two other fungi I like because they are tasty, common, and safe are puffballs—white or light tan, solid, round or ovoid masses—and bracket fungi, those brown to orange, or even red, "shelves" you sometimes see attached to dead trees. My resources and authorities tell me that all puffballs and bracket fungi are edible; I'm still leery, though, and before I'd eat anything, I'd want to check it against a reliable

More about Mushrooms

My technique for preparing inky caps or shaggymanes is the essence of simplicity. I rinse them and throw them into a buttered pan, briefly sautéing them, and that's it. They throw off a dark liquid as they are cooking—don't be surprised or dismayed. They just do that.

Inky Cap Pot

2 pounds clean *Coprinus* mushrooms (as you pick them, nip off the dirty bases so the dirt doesn't fall into the gills of other mushrooms in your sack or basket)

1 large or 2 small eggs

⅓ cup butter (okay, okay . . . or margarine)

2 cups dry bread crumbs, crushed cornflakes, or croutons

Sauté the mushrooms in butter until the juice runs freely. Add the beaten egg(s) and enough crumbs to sop up the mushroom juice. Season to taste with salt and pepper and bake at 350 degrees for about a quarter hour.

mushroom guide with illustrations and a guide if at all possible. In the Italian community of Omaha, Nebraska, it is the "beefsteak" bracket mushroom that is most sought after;

invasions of other families' hunting grounds have ignited lifelong, furious feuds. Once bracket mushrooms grow old, they get as hard as the wood they are attached to, so while they all may be edible, they're not all palatable. In the case of puffballs, be sure once you cut them open that there are no signs of a stem inside; if so, you may be dealing with an immature mushroom rather than a puffball, and it may be a dangerous one.

Moreover, you want to be sure you have very young puffballs. They spring up overnight to the size of Ping-Pong balls or footballs and are quickly beset with little worms, which also apparently like mushrooms. The puffballs quickly mature and become, well, *puff*balls. They get brown and tough and pretty soon are nothing more than leathery little pouches that, when touched, "puff" out "puffs" of what looks like smoke . . . but is actually reproductive spores. Kids love mature puffballs because they are like miniature bombs. Plains Indians used the powdery contents of puffballs as a styptic to stop bleeding in minor wounds.

If you are looking for puffballs to eat, select only those that are fresh, white through and through, firm, and, uh, unoccupied.

Fungi are for some gourmets the only wild food they pursue. And that's fine. There are many, many other excellent mushrooms free for the picking. The distinctive sulfur mushroom, for example, is pink to tan on the top and sulfur yellow on the bottom; it grows in large clumps in the late summer and early fall on hardwoods, especially oak. The winter mushroom has a yellow-brown sticky-wet cap and prefers elm trees. Still, the most useful trait it has is that it grows in the dead of the winter, when there are few other mushrooms around with which it might be confused and when there aren't many other wild foods for the avid forager.

Smut

I'm going to wander just a touch off the track here. I have advertised this book as being about wild foods—plants that grow wild, in the wild. Well, after morels, my favorite fungus isn't really wild at all, and can't be found anywhere except in cultivated crops—although the crop in question is *not* the mushroom itself. Doesn't that sound mysterious? It gets even better.

There is no such thing as wild corn. Corn has been a part of human society for so long, it is now inextricably bound to us. No wonder many Plains Indian tribes considered corn their mother deity. For them, without corn there would be no human life; and marvelously, conversely, without human life, there would be no corn.

Corn suffers an affliction, however, called smut. Say it: "smut." Doesn't that just roll off your tongue? Smut smut smut smut. It's a bluish fungus that grows on corn ears and looks kind of terrible, if you think too much about it. It looks like huge, bloated, blue kernels of the corn swelling out of the cob. Ick. And of course there's that unfortunate moniker—smut smut smut.

But Plains Indians didn't consider smut a curse at all. In fact, they rather liked it. Actually, they celebrated it. "Oh, boy, look here! I just found some smut! It looks like maybe a lot of our corn is going to be blessed with smut this year! God is good!" Yellowed ethnologies tell me that before the white man came along and taught them that smut was icky, the Indians boiled it up and thoroughly enjoyed it. It is, after all, a mushroom! So one day many years ago I noticed that our neighbors across the road had a large patch of sweet corn coming along, and many ears showed an infection of— smut! When I asked them if I could take some of the ears that were so blighted, they looked at me kind of funny (as they have since come to do with frequency) and said, uh, well, uh, I suppose . . . okay. And I set out with a five-gallon bucket and a cheerful heart and gathered a load of smut.

I cooked it up, and as I have so often found when it comes to Indian food, it was delicious! Slightly mushroomy, slightly corny—a lovely, delicate combination of two wonderful tastes. Sure, it was blue and kind of ugly for that reason, but if you didn't look too close . . .

For many years thereafter I joked that somebody was going to get rich if they simply figured out how to propagate and encourage smut, harvested it, packed it, and, most importantly of all, came up with a good name for it. Something French, maybe. Something that sounds gourmet. Truffles de Maize, for example. Or Bleu-Des-Gustin.

Next thing I knew, someone had done exactly that. They were harvesting smut in Mexico, packaging it, and selling it as a Mayan delicacy. They even had come up with a fancy name for it—*huitlacoche*. I don't like to talk about it because all I can think is how close I came to being a smut mogul . . . if only I'd had the capital.

Tasty Ways with Smut

And don't you just love saying it? Be sure the smut you get is fresh and firm, not soggy, powdery, or wormy. (Worms know a good thing when it comes along!) I boil my smut, but I'm thinking that the next time I'm lucky enough to find some, I'm going to steam it. Like any mushroom, it doesn't take a lot of time to cook it through. I have never mixed my smut with anything else (but wouldn't it be fun to put together a menu of smut with butt steak or lamb shank, sweet potatoes, cheesecake—almost certainly cherry—and G-string beans?), simply serving it as a side dish to any meat with which something tasting faintly of corn and mushrooms would go well. For sentimental reasons, I suppose, we like it with buffalo meat, but then we eat mostly buffalo here anyway. We really prefer it and buy from a bison herd just a couple of miles upstream. Linda says that she is so drawn to buffalo meat, she can't help but wonder if maybe in a previous life she wasn't carried off into the harsh wilderness by some brutal savage who kept her as his housekeeper and sex slave . . . "sort of like now."

Steam or boil your smut, drain, and salt lightly. We have occasionally had some fairly dry smut and find that a smear of butter really improves it, as it would any sweet corn.

So you don't even have to go out into the woods to find good fungus delicacies for your gourmet meals; watch your garden sweet corn, check on your neighbors, ask around to see if anyone knows where you can get some smut. You may want to keep this book handy, however, in the event that you have to explain all this to the local morality police. (For more information, an excellent Web site is http://www.halfmoon .org/story/smut.html.)

Mushroom Kits

I can't remember how we used to find information before the World Wide Web came along. I know that I found mushroom kits for sale in classified ads in *Natural History* magazine when I was writing a column for that fine magazine. I ordered them and found them easy, clean, and successful. I simply put the boxes under our laundry room sink, followed instructions, and then for a couple of weeks we ate high off the hog. These days there are a lot more sources for mushroom kits, a richer variety of mushrooms, better prices, and a lot of places to find them, simply by typing in "mushroom growing kits" into Google or any other search machine. I just took a quick look and found several places that look like great sources if you would like to skip the troubles (okay, and joys) and risks of hunting wild mushrooms. Heaven only knows how much things will change by the time you see this page, so I recommend that you go to Google yourself—if there still is a Google. But for starters or for those of you who aren't online, consider the following:

Peaceful Valley Farm Supply
P.O. Box 2209
Grass Valley, CA 95945
(530) 272–4769
www.groworganic.com

Gourmet Mushroom Products
P.O. Box 515 IP
Graton, CA 95444
(707) 829–7301
www.gmushrooms.com/pots.htm

Chapter Seven

GREENS AND VEGETABLES

Nature knows no difference between weeds and flowers.

—Mason Cooley

Ick. Greens and vegetables. Who likes greens and vegetables? Well, you would, if you served fresh greens and vegetables, interesting greens and vegetables, or, better yet, outrageous greens and vegetables. For example, grocery store lettuce is okay—I like a salad with grocery store lettuce. But even more, I like a salad with fresh, crispy, dark green spinach rather than the pallid, whitish, tasteless stuff that's harvested and shipped 1,000 miles these days. And maybe a little zingy watercress in there, too, huh? Now you're talking. That's not just some kind of fern-bar ladies' dish . . . that's *food*.

Salad Days

You can enjoy all this if you gather wild greens for your table—maybe not for every meal, but now and then. I once tagged along on a packaged canoeing expedition as a campfire entertainer, playing my banjo and talking about the history of the area. But as usual, I wound up annoying the bejeezus out of the camp cooks by altering their pat formula recipes by adding wild foods to dishes they were already working on or by coming up with something altogether different as a substitute. When they served iceberg lettuce salad, for example, I pulled a few hands of tart watercress from along the riverbank, rinsed it, cut it up just a bit, and tossed it into their huge salad washtub. They were convinced I had spoiled their recipe. The eaters made it clear I had not—they gobbled it up, digging around especially for those little morsels of . . . "What is that anyway? Where did you find this stuff? Man, is that ever good!" When I showed them where it was growing along the banks of the river, they couldn't believe it: The best stuff was the free stuff!

Like watercress, daylily flower buds give zest to salads, and the twisty remnants of yesterday's daylily blooms do the same for soup. Kids love this notion of eating weeds—to their mind it's a minor defiance, a gesture of protest, a departure from what's right, an indulgence in a no-no: "You kids quit eating those weeds! God only knows what that stuff is! If you poison yourselves and die, don't come running to me!" A small handful of oxalis—the stuff your kids probably call "lollipops" and already know are tart edibles that they munch on every day on the way to school in the spring and autumn—will add zest and interest to any salad. They look like little folded clover leaves and have tiny five-petaled, brilliant yellow flowers. They taste just a bit like a delicate rhubarb. Yum! Throw a handful of these into any pedestrian salad and you'll have guests asking what the heck you did to make that salad so zesty: "What are these little shamrocky things that taste so good?" Tell them you found Belgian Vert du Pays at a very chichi gourmet specialty store. What do they know?

Most wild greens are best picked young, as is the case with any green for the table. If you let lettuce go very far along the line toward maturation, it quickly becomes a shrubby mess of woody leaves and stiff veins. Heck, you might just as well be eating weeds! Especially if the weeds are young and fresh. A good indicator is the flowers or seed stems: When they've stabbed up from the crown or center of the plant, chances are it's too late for that particular plant to be picked for a salad. With dandelion greens, an old classic for the salad bowl, once the flower stem sticks up with its gorgeous yellow blossom, you can pretty much write off the greens as milky, coarse, and acrid to the palate.

If there is a problem with wild greens, it's that they tend to be quite small. You could, in fact, argue that it's a lot easier to gather a head of pale, insipid lettuce off a grocery produce shelf than to pick a handful of greens from the weeds around the patio.

But this doesn't hold much water with me. I find that you don't need quite as many wild greens as domestic for a decent salad; because of their rich color and taste, they seem to be more filling. Too, it's not really that much trouble—it takes only a minute or two to pick a small handful of greens unless you're preparing a major banquet.

Still, if the labor is a problem for you, take advantage of that time of the year—late April, usually—when sour dock is young and ready for the table. Its leaves are big, and it doesn't take many at all to fill a salad bowl. As the name suggests, sour dock has a nice tang to it, too—not really a bitterness, but just the sort of zip you expect and enjoy with a salad under an oil and vinegar (vinegar!) dressing.

Boiled Greens

"Eat your boiled greens and shut up." Ick. No one likes that canned stuff that looks for all the world like a dirty washrag. And there's a reason for that: A boiled dirty washrag would taste better than this slop. I have no intention of telling you that you have to eat this stuff or that you won't get any dessert. Not even if you are marooned and starving in the Kansas jungles do you need to eat bad food. Wild greens and vegetables, when prepared right, are not just tolerable; they are superb. They are a delicacy . . . a gourmet treat.

The same is true even with salads. I do like crisp lettuce or spinach in a salad, with some watercress for zest. But even in the best restaurant or grocery store, that greenery has probably been on the road in a refrigerated truck for three or four days before it gets to your plate. How much better anything is when it is only instants from the picking, steamed for just a moment instead of boiled into a ropy mess, crunchy, fresh, filled with vitamins and yummies.

Cooking Greens

Greens: horseradish, dock, mustard, anything tart and/or strong

Recipe 1: Sauté a slice or two of bacon or salt pork, remove from the pan, add one to two bunches of chopped cold greens to the grease, and stir until the greens wilt. Lower the heat, cover, and steam for about four minutes. Check the seasoning and add salt and fresh-ground pepper. This is wonderful with scraps of meat from a previous meal or sliced or crumbled hard-boiled eggs.

Recipe 2: Wash the greens, shake, chop, and put into a covered saucepan. Steam in the water remaining on the leaves until tender—about four minutes. Less is better. Season with salt, butter, and pepper. Remember that greens reduce a lot when cooked, so start with plenty— like two quarts for six servings. Throw in some wild onions, chives, peppergrass, or wild mustard for a really tangy dish.

A Mess o' Greens

Just look around you the next time you drive down a country road. What do you see? *Green!* And a lot of that is edible— even choice. As idiotic as it sounds, there is also something to getting food free, and eating wild stuff, and eating stuff no one else is eating. This goes double for kids.

Plantain

Plantain is easily identified and plentiful. It is sometimes called "Englishman's foot" because the world had the distinct impression—in large part true!—that wherever an English adventurer, soldier, or sailor planted his foot, danged if plantain didn't spring up. My bet is that if you send the shoes you have on at this moment into a lab for analysis, the report will come back that in the cracks and faint traces of dirt in the tread there were plaintain seeds.

While this plant is in the same family as the tropical plantain you enjoyed fried in the Yucatan or Jamaica, a small, stiffer, more flavorful banana, unfortunately this is an untamed, smaller, less fruitful variety. But if you look at the erect seed stalks, you will definitely note a resemblance to a "hand" or stalk of agricultural bananas.

Young, tender plantain leaves are excellent for salads and greens, looking for all the world like slightly greener and more nutritious spinach leaves. However, they are also excellent for breaded fritters. Prepare a stiff batter of milk, egg, and cracker or dry bread crumbs. Fry over a low heat for fifteen to thirty minutes or less.

Wildflowers

I am even more enthusiastic about wild violets. They are just like domesticated variety, with slightly less dramatic flowers and smaller leaves. But the leaves are still heart shaped, the flowers a delicate blue, and they are tasty.

There was a time when I considered my strong attraction to flowers as edibles a bit, well, strange. I mentioned this to Charles Kuralt, the CBS newsman and one of the nicest guys I have known in this long life. We were eating a daylily salad at the time, garnished with the orange flowers. Charles thought about it a moment and then said, in a private sort of way, "Well, sure, Rog. They are, after all, the plants' sex organs." Somehow, since that day I've never felt quite the same about eating flowers.

Fiddleheads

Even here on the Great Plains and definitely to the east, a woodland just isn't complete without brackens or wild ferns—sometimes called fiddleheads, because that's exactly what they look like. They are sometimes listed as being poisonous, and when cattle, or maybe even people, eat them in quantity they can be. But I've eaten my fill of them and never had any trouble. You may want to try them with some caution, however, until you know how your system handles the digestion of this plant.

That little rolled-up frond that becomes the fern's "leaf" is what you're looking for. It is excellent eaten just as it is, but I prefer them boiled or steamed lightly and served with a pat of butter or bacon grease.

Pigweed

Pigweeds (a term most often applied to the goosefoot family, or *Chenopodium*—which is Latin for "goose foot" because the leaves look like, well, goose feet) are very common, easily identified, widely distributed, long lasting (through the summer), delicious, and nutritious. Pick a mess from your

Bacon Grease

The world is currently beset with various experts, dietitians, and diet gurus who all have bad things to say about bacon grease, just as surely as there is some self-appointed guardian ready to condemn just about anything else worth eating. Thing is, when you're out camping, you will probably have some bacon, salt pork, or fatback along, and it would be wasteful and foolish not to take advantage of the melted condiment left in the frying pan after breakfast. It is wonderful on any greens—lamb's-quarters, purslane, wild vegetables, dandelion crowns, Cossack asparagus, asparagus per se, poke, even delicacies like morels.

I was once encamped with a dear Lakota friend of mine on the Rosebud reservation, and his aunt invited us into her lodge for sweet corn. It was Sun Dance time and we were on the Rosebud powwow grounds. I love sweet corn, with a bit of salt and butter, but this time I was surprised because the corn was served (and quite clearly this was the usual way for the family) with a dab of bacon grease on it. It was perfectly delicious. If I hadn't already been a fan of bacon, that would have done it for me.

yard or fence, rinse them off, tear them up, toss them in a bowl, and you have salad.

Or you can cook them, especially the pigweed known as lamb's-quarters. Pick young tender shoots and topmost leaves. Drop them for just a short minute into boiling water. As with all greens, lamb's-quarters profits from just a bit of salt and fat. A pat of genuine butter is perfect, but—especially in camp, where supplies might be short—a bit of game fat, salt pork, bacon, or pemmican does the job very nicely as well. I fry the fat or bacon in the bottom of a pot and then dump a little water and the cleaned greens right into the same container, saving any loss of fat and saving one dish come time to wash up. In our family we call them "greasy greens," a compliment . . . maybe even a term of affection. Lamb's-quarters is a widely used green because it is so good. Gather plenty, because it cooks down a good deal.

Pokeweed

I've already mentioned pokeweed (aka poke salad, or salat) because it's pretty hard for me to talk about edible wild foods without mentioning poke. There simply is nothing better than poke greens. Nothing. If you offered me at this very moment an eight-ounce filet mignon wrapped in bacon and cooked over mesquite, rare, or the equivalent amount of freshly picked poke steamed for five minutes and dabbed with butter—real butter, mind, because we're talking a major trade-off here—I'd take the poke. It's that good. And it gets better in my mind every year the farther we get away from May and poke season. That is truly one of the delights of opportunist food gathering. You have the long anticipation of the wonderful food before its season arrives. Then you have the brief but orgiastic time when it is on the table every day. And finally you have warm memories of when something so good was so plentiful . . . and now you can start anticipating again. I'm that way about bacon, lettuce, and tomato sandwiches too. I have tried to talk Linda into a scientific experiment where we eat BLTs every day for as long a period as we can until we actually say, "Enough! No more!" I'm betting the end of one BLT season would thus run right into the beginning of the next. I cannot imagine getting tired of bacon, lettuce, and tomato sandwiches.

To my mind and palate, poke is in the same category as bacon, lettuce, and tomato sandwiches. And as asparagus . . . thick thumb-size spears stabbing up in early spring, snapped off and popped into a pot of boiling water or steamed just long enough to make them even more tender, and then shoveled generously onto a plate with plenty of butter—oh, my! And as is the case with asparagus, it's a real mistake to go out into the field looking for poke about the time it's ready to pick and you have developed a winter-long appetite for it. You'll never find those elusive spears that way. Little wonder the Sainted Euell Gibbons called his first book for weed seekers *Stalking the Wild Asparagus*. Aside from the clever pun on asparagus *stalks*, there is definitely an allegorical allusion to the very real fact that if you intend to enjoy such delicacies, you must pursue them with the stealth and forethought used by the most accomplished big-game hunter.

No, if you intend to enjoy asparagus or poke, you must think ahead. Watch for the tall stalks of large-leafed poke during the summer when it is in full growth—and, incidentally, poisonous. Look for the bunches of large, deep purple, loosely gathered berries. Find someone who can tell you for sure if this is poke, or take a sample to a botanist, extension service officer, naturalist, or avid weed eater for identification.

By the way, if you are going to ask other weed eaters about such things, the best idea is to take a sample to them rather than taking them to your find; otherwise, when you go there next spring to harvest your poke, you are liable to find ragged stumps and footprints that look for all the world like the sneakers your friend was wearing last summer when you brought her here for positive identification of what you thought might be pokeweed. All things are fair in love, war, and poke salad.

Poke looks like asparagus, is picked like asparagus, and is prepared for the table like asparagus. The tender young spears are snapped off at their base and carried to the cooking pot as quickly as possible. The spears can be boiled directly in the water or steamed above it until tender—just a few minutes. Butter, bacon grease, and a bit of salt are all you need to make yourself a mess of the finest fixin's you have ever had in your life. There is a reason people, especially in this nation's Southeast, sing songs and write poetry about "poke salat," as it is pronounced and spelled there. It's simply that good. Once you taste poke, you won't forget it and you will never again pass by a mature patch without making a mental note that you just have to get back there the next May when the sprouts are poking 6 or 8 inches above the wet and cool soil.

Prickly Pear

While many plants are much better food than prickly pear, nothing is more satisfying steaming and ready to eat on my plate. My sixty-acre patch here in central Nebraska is infested with prickly pear cactus. It is wretched stuff and, insofar as I can tell, virtually impossible to eradicate. I have sprayed, burned, salted, and peed on prickly pear, and my impression is that if it could, it would dance around in glee and beg for more of my fond attention. It is also called "jumping cactus" because it seems for all the world that that's what it does. You can be walking along perfectly innocently and avoiding prickly pear cacti by never passing closer than 15 yards from them, and yet in your first unguarded moment you will feel the stinging pain of an entire pad of the miserable, wretched stuff embedding itself into some vulnerable and presumably inaccessible part of your flesh. Once you have pulled the pad off, there are still spines sticking into your flesh. And even after you have pulled out the individual spines—all of them—for weeks you will find little irritating hairs stuck in your flesh, pustulating and swelling. Prickly pear cactus is a curse.

So imagine if you can the feelings of those of us who have suffered from the aggressions of this plague when we see a steaming pile of its cursed flesh on our plates, having died a horrible death by scalding, and now about to be devoured in the ultimate vengeful act: nourishing us, the very flesh it would have tortured!

Long before I owned this sand pile I call home, I was walking through a wonderful market in Monterrey, Mexico, early one morning and saw a woman sitting beside a pile of gigantic prickly pear cactus pads. (Not the pears themselves, the fruit of the cactus flower, but the pads of the plant. More about the pears later.) I stopped and with my ten-word Spanish vocabulary and her better but still modest English, I managed to communicate that I wondered what the heck she was going to do with her cactus. She shaved a few fleshy strips from the pads on the floor beside her, cleaned off their spines, and with gestures invited me to taste them. Hmmm . . . not an exciting taste, but not unpleasant, either. Another woman from a booth not far away, in a generous gesture I have found to be typical of the Mexican people, came rushing over with a cup of soup she was cooking for sale, containing what were clearly strips of cactus! Very good . . . and, I later learned, a wonderful thickener to make a hearty soup even more muscular. On the way back to my hotel room at noon, I then noticed and understood those gigantic, groaning wagons of prickly pear cactus pads, heading toward the market and the nation's soup pots.

Just two days ago in a grocery store in the increasingly Hispanic town of Grand Island, Nebraska, I nudged Wife Linda and pointed to a pile of prickly pear on a specialty counter, right between the jicama and smoked, dried peppers. It's no longer exotic; prickly pear is now a staple here, too.

Up to now I have been talking about the cactus itself, also called beaver tail because that's what this cactus looks like. But the reason it's called prickly *pear* is that after the plant throws up its lush yellow or white blossoms in the spring, it develops fleshy, globulose, purplish fruits that some people relish as a base for jelly. Frankly, I consider the fruits the least interesting foodstuffs of the plant. Friend and plant expert Kay Young has told me that she has found *spineless* prickly pear fruits, and that certainly would make it more attractive, but so far I haven't been that lucky. The whole plant hates me with a fury. I can't deal with it without coming away injured. Not even leather gloves protect me from damage. Maybe I'm just delicate. Uh-huh, yeah.

When I go through the trouble of eating homegrown prickly pears, I pick them with metal tongs and carry them in glass or crockery bowls. In my case anything else—even plastic or wood—simply collects and reserves the spines for later self-inflicted wounds. Then, still with the tongs or metal skewers, I hold and turn the pads over a flame to burn off as many of the spines as I can. Still holding the pads with tongs, I scrape across the pods with a sharp knife, and the tufts of spines come right off.

Commercially available prickly pear pads, imported from the Southwest or Mexico, don't carry with them the emotional gratification of striking back at Satan's Spawn gathered for my own grand and personal revenge, but they are definitely easier to deal with since they are much larger than the wild variety and also have much more widely spaced and less malicious spine clusters. The cactus pads we buy here in our grocery stores have the spines already burned off—a real convenience. I would recommend that for the satisfaction of fighting evil you should eat wild prickly pear; for gustatory gratification, however, settle for the domesticated stuff you can buy in the Mexican foods section

Preparing Prickly Pear

To burn the spines off prickly pear pads, simply hold the pads briefly over flames until there's nothing but charred spots left. Then place the pads on a firm base—a board, canoe bottom, whatever—and scrape with a sharp knife, so the sharp edge of the blade is forward. Don't cut into the flesh of the cactus. The charred burn spots will come right off. Rinse the cactus pads and slice them into sections about the size of a green bean. These can be eaten raw; they have a nice "al dente" texture, a touch slimy but not offensively so, a fresh "vegetable taste" a bit to me like asparagus. Or put the cleaned strips into soup—a super addition for texture and flavor, and the nice green looks good, too. Or boil or steam a bunch of the strips as a side-dish vegetable. A pad of butter or bacon grease and a sprinkle of salt and I think you will be quite pleased with this new addition to an elegant dinner or a campfire tin-pan meal.

My favorite way to eat prickly pear came to me as something of a surprise. I was grilling some steaks over a campfire and had found some large prickly pear cactus pads not far from camp—not only a nice gustatory addition but a great conversation piece for my campmates, who weren't all that familiar with grazing in the countryside. I tossed five or six large pads on the grill near the steaks, figuring I'd burn off the spines, scrape the pads, and . . . oh, I don't know, maybe slice them up and boil them for a vegetable, I suppose, or add raw strips to whatever greens I could find for a salad.

Well, what with the good conversation, a cup or two of good bourbon, and the attention I paid to the meat on the fire, I lost track of the cactus pads. The spines burned off okay, but I left the pads on the fire too long and they cooked over the coals. That complicated scraping them because they were now softened by the cooking, but I did what I could. There wasn't much left to scrape because the spines were pretty much taken care of by the fire. I rinsed the pads with clean water and sliced them up, still not sure whether I was going to boil or steam the pads or throw them into a soup.

Then I tasted one of the strips. Wow! Was that ever good! The touch of smoke really added something lovely to the dish. So I just sliced up my broiled cactus and served it as a vegetable along with the steaks. I was not alone in my enthusiasm for this new discovery. I *highly* recommend this way of cooking prickly pear for your dining room or campfire meal.

Or how about this? Sear, scrape, and clean your prickly pear pads. Then cut them into bite-size pieces and add them to your shish kebab skewer along with whatever else you have on there—meat, potatoes, peppers . . . Again, it is not simply the very pleasant flavor of cactus but also the color and texture that recommend prickly pear in this kind of preparation. I'm betting you'll make prickly pear a regular addition to your grilling choices—to the amazement of your family and guests!

of your supermarket. And while you're there, pick up one of those huge, light brown roots called jicama. Wash it off, peel it, slice it up, and eat it raw. Yum yum! And my thanks to our new Hispanic citizens!

Actually, a lot of wild plant foods are increasingly available as specialties or novelties in supermarkets: Jerusalem artichokes, ground cherries, and prickly pear cactus, most notably. They tend to be larger versions of what you find in the wild, but they are clearly the same plant. I think that is a clear underscoring of my constant point in these pages: The foods I am talking about are not simply handy to know about as survival foods but actually good enough to consider for appearances on your regular supper table.

I don't think of buying commercially available "weeds" as cheating. In fact, I recommend that you buy the commercial products in the grocery store when you simply want something good for your table or would like to see if a plant is worth the time and trouble of gathering in the wild. And of course, then you will know how to handle the same plant for fun or fare in the wild.

Chapter Eight
IT'S THE BERRIES

O thou weed!
Who art so lovely fair and smell'st
so sweet
That the sense aches at thee . . .
—Shakespeare, *Othello*

You'd better sit down for this one. I'm about to tell you a story, and it's a long one.

I came to the notion of wild foods from a lot of different directions. There was my association with Native Americans, my interest in regionalism (the Plains), and a burning obsession with making my own wine. I started with no knowledge of the science of winemaking —oenology, as it's called by the highfalutin—whatsoever. I guess we all start just about anything with no knowledge. That's the nature of learning, after all. But at the time I started, there were precious few books available on the process, while now the shelves groan under the weight of winemaking books. There were no winemaker's supply stores, either. Eventually I started one and supported my own habit by selling supplies to others, soon even brokering large shipments of wine grapes from California to amateur Nebraska winemakers.

Among winemakers there is a popular story about the Italian vintner who is dying and calls his sons to his bedside. He signals them to bend low, putting their ears close to his mouth, and he tells them that he is about to reveal to them the true secret of his winemaking skills. "It . . . can . . . it can . . . ," he mutters with great effort. "It . . . can . . . also . . . be made . . . from grapes!"

The moral of that story is, you can make wine from anything. Not great wine, to be sure. In fact, not even good wine. But you can make *drinkable* wine from just about anything. And for many years in many places for many people, if you wanted wine, you just about had to make it from anything. Grapes native to America are not wine grapes. They are a completely different thing. Wine made from American labrusca grapes are "foxy," which in the case of wines is not good. The only way wine made from American native grapes can be made drinkable is to make it very sweet.

Early in our history efforts were made to bring European *wine* grapes to this continent, but a couple of terrible diseases struck, wiping out the wine grape crop here—and then they were accidentally carried back to Europe, where they wreaked even more havoc. We actually came within a whisker of losing real wine forever. I know, horrible, horrible thought . . . it gives me the shivers, too. I won't go into the biology and technology of the matter, but European grapes were saved, pretty much, and now wonderful hybrids have been developed for almost all geographies in this hemisphere; you can get locally made, excellent wines just about everywhere. A heartwarming ending to what could have been a terrible tragedy.

But for a long time, winemaking wasn't easy in the New World. German migrants to this country worked hard at imitating the light, tart white wines of their homeland with bases like rhubarb, and did pretty well at it. Italians did what they could to manufacture passable reds with wild grapes, or elderberries. Others tried dandelion flowers, chokecherries, peaches, whatever they could find.

And that's what I did, too, when I got started in the hobby forty years ago. I had an uncle at the time who worked in a wholesale produce warehouse. Every Friday, when they got ready to discard any fruit that was approaching a no-longer-saleable condition, there I was at the loading dock, loading lugs of whatever they had: peaches, apricots, Thompson seedless grapes, cherries, strawberries . . . I hauled it home and did what I could to make wine out of it. Some of my final products were terrible, but enough was passable to keep me going, and occasionally some of it was superb, which made me all the more eager to learn more and do better.

I learned that you can never make decent wine, for example, with bread yeast as the fermenter, or by counting on the yeasts that gather naturally on fruit skins. (You know that grayish haze on dark grapes or plums? That's yeast. It's everywhere, lusting to get inside that skin to the sugars it will then eat and convert—a nice word for "pee"—back as alcohol.) I eventually learned to test for just the right amount of sugars so the wine didn't wind up cloyingly sweet or continue to ferment in the bottle and explode in our basement . . . always between two and three in the morning.

And I learned that "it can also . . . be made from grapes." Wine grapes. I bought tons—railcars—of true wine grapes from California and resold them to other winemakers in my hometown of Lincoln, Nebraska. I know the following story is already way too long for a book about *wild* foods, but this opportunity (1) is too good to pass up, and (2) does basically deal with the virtues of gathering and salvage. I guess. It also proves the existence of God—no small matter, after all.

One evening I was collapsed in my chair watching the evening news. I was exhausted because that very day I had received, processed, stemmed, and crushed a huge shipment of grapes from California—zinfandels, as I recall. And I was a trifle unsettled because I wound up with just a hundred pounds or so too few grapes to fill my barrels. It's not good to have too little wine aging in a barrel—too much air can spoil a wine. So even while I was catching up on the news, I was mulling over what I was going to do about quickly acquiring more grapes to top up my vats without watering down the purity of my 100 percent zinfandel wine.

There was the weather report . . . nothing new there. Some minor crimes in the area . . . boring. A train wreck at a town 50 miles to the north . . . hmmm . . . wow. What a mess. Lumber everywhere. Bags of agricultural lime scattered around. A carload of what looked like gravel or sand. Oh, well, that happens, and it has nothing to do with me and my problems. And there were a bunch of boxes of . . . can't tell . . . something . . . something kind of purplish . . . *something that looks for all the world like zinfandel grapes!*

Now, that simply was not possible. No, it would be *insane* for me to be sitting there in desperate need of zinfandel grapes and for a trainload of zinfandels to be dropped into my lap by a train wreck. No one is that lucky! Not the guys who win the lottery, not the guys who are saved from a bullet by a Bible in their shirt pocket, not the guys who have slept with Cindy Crawford . . . no one is *that* lucky! No god is that generous!

The camera panned the scene of the wreckage again, and the color was unmistakable to my practiced eye. They were grapes, and they were zinfandel grapes. I could even tell that at the distance of 50 miles and through a camera's lens, lit by a puny light, at night.

I had a winemaking friend in the same town where the train had derailed. I called him, and he was already sputtering so bad we couldn't have a decent conversation. He had seen the news report, too, and he was headed to his car to get to the wreck and see if we could salvage those grapes. Fifteen minutes later he called back. He had found the wreck, he had talked with the officials on the scene. They said it was strictly illegal to salvage before law enforcement arrived on the scene—in a couple of days. They also didn't want anyone scrounging around in wreckage where they might get hurt. And any salvage without official authorization was also against company policy, he said.

Damn. End of story. No grapes for us.

But as my friend walked dejectedly back to his car, he noticed some railroad workers moving furtively in the dark back behind some of the wrecked cars. They were moving hundreds of lugs of undamaged zinfandel grapes from the upset cars to a hidden place behind a railroad building not far from the wreck and stacking them nicely for later retrieval when they got off work.

Moral Dilemma: Is it really a crime to steal from thieves? We discussed this ethical issue maybe three seconds before concluding, "Hell no! These guys deserve a lesson in the folly of their sinful ways!" My friend dashed back out to his car as I dashed out to mine. We grabbed handfuls of mud and covered parts of our vehicles, most especially the license plates. Lights dimmed, we rolled quietly up behind the railroad building where there were now hundreds of neatly stacked cases of undamaged zinfandels. Quickly, quietly we loaded our vans to the point that the springs were groaning and threatening collapse. Quietly we rolled back into the dark night.

I don't think we slept that night, we were so utterly gleeful. God had smiled on us. He had used us to punish the unworthy. We had committed the truly victimless crime— The Grape Train Robbery. And the next day we had barrels more of excellent wine at a price you simply cannot beat.

And even better, we had a story to tell our children.

A Perfect Abundance

Finding an abundance of free wild food is a lot like that, except without the glaring moral righteousness. A friend and I were once out looking for wild grapes near the east end of the Mormon Bridge where it crosses into Iowa from Omaha. We were doing fine. We had a bushel or so each of these deep navy-blue berries. We would have a couple of gallons of really nice wine, close to an excellent port if we did everything right with our harvest. Then we stumbled into a clearing near a Missouri River backwater and there for all the world was a sight that might just as well have been the Garden of Eden. In the middle of a dramatic open spot in the woods was a huge old cottonwood, weighted down with a drapery of wild grapevines carrying—literally—tons of wild grapes in beautiful, tight, perfectly ripe, clean clusters. We simply couldn't believe our eyes. We picked everything within reach. Then we stood on the roof of my old battered Chevy van and picked more. We had hundreds and hundreds of pounds of perfect wild grapes.

Now, wild grapes are native American grapes, labruscas—jelly and juice grapes—rather than viniferas, or wine grapes. But I found that when blended with elderberries and a bit of water, they make a superb, portlike wine. Elderberries are too blah for decent wine—not enough acid—but wild grapes are a touch too acidic, if anything. So the combination is perfect, producing a heavy, velvety, dark red wine. Yummy! How many grapes to how many elderberries? Again, making things like wine or omelets is not a matter of following a formula. For one thing, tastes differ. For another, the depth of flavor, the amount of acid, the intensity of color, blah blah blah, all differ from plant to plant, region to region, year to year . . . in fact, yard to yard and day to day. You need to judge for yourself for your own taste and build up experience that will give you the judgment to make decisions dependent on what you have there on the table before you.

So where are you going to find *your* Tree of Knowledge? When I first got started in winemaking and in wild foods, a neighbor came by to share some of a mess of wild plums she had picked along a country road. They were delicious, sweet and juicy, and my interest was fired. I wanted to pick some wild plums. "Where were these plums?" I asked.

Our neighbor was at a loss how to answer. The plums were in a thicket. Along a country road. She didn't know where exactly. Well, could she give me some idea where to look? Not really. At the time I was baffled how she could be so confused about something so simple. Where did she find the plums? Couldn't she have just said something like "Ten miles east of Ong," or something like that?

I quickly learned what the problem was: Wild plums are everywhere. It was as if I had asked, "Where can I see some mashed potatoes? I am really curious about them and would love to see what they look like?" Where would I find mashed potatoes? Well, on a plate in a diner, I suppose! It's not as if mashed potatoes are a rare commodity. Same with wild plums. They are virtually everywhere. You can't drive a mile on a country road in Nebraska (and probably elsewhere) without passing a plum thicket. The problem is that I had never looked for a plum thicket, and I didn't know what to look for. A week or so later, I had the good fortune (!) of having a flat tire on a highway in the countryside, and of course everywhere around me were plum thickets, heavy with sweet, ripe plums. Once you know what to look for, the question of where to look becomes secondary. We're talking about wild plants, for Pete's sake! That means . . . *they are wild!* They grow anywhere and everywhere. If you learn the time of year when the fruit is likely to be ripe, your bushel baskets will soon be full of free, delicious, nutritious food.

However, there *are* times to look for wild foods other than when they are ripe. In fact, it is better in many, maybe *most*, cases to look for wild fruits when they are not ready to be picked. Learn to recognize the tall, feathery, yellow to light brown fronds of last year's asparagus, for example. Then as you drive along you will easily spot where to look next April for the short, tender, green shoots. (I sometimes tie a small tag of brightly colored tape to a fence or post to remind me exactly where I should be on my hands and knees next spring.) A grapevine covered with snow, but showing the dried raisins of last year's growth, is a signal that this is a spot to check next August. In the early spring I watch for the easily distinguished flowers of the plum bush, saving me peering into heavy foliage a couple of months later for the dark fruit that may not be easily seen when ripe. As I drive along a week or two later, I watch for the clustered, fragrant flowers of chokecherries so I know where to look in mid-July for the black fruit. Last year's cattails tell me where to find this year's. In some cases you won't even have to use your eyes: once you learn to recognize the rich, heavy perfume of elderblow (for reasons I have never heard, the flower of the elderberry is called "blow"); you will only need to follow the scent a few yards upwind to find the huge, ivory flower heads where a month later there will be gigantic, heavy heads of berries.

If the ultimate goal and pleasure of gathering wild fruits and berries is in the eating, you still cannot and should not dismiss the pleasures of gathering the bounty. I don't care if it's simply a matter of walking along, spotting a mulberry bush loaded with black or white berries, grabbing a handful without so much as slowing down, and munching on the go, or making a deliberate expedition to a chokecherry thicket or elderberry marsh to gather bushel baskets full for later days of processing into jellies, pies, juices, and wine. There is nothing like the satisfaction of delicious goodies for nothing—a gift of the gods, better than the pallid fruits everyone else is enjoying from the supermarket. And yes, you'll be apologizing for those stained hands and arms—and lips—for weeks, but you'll also be eating the pies and ice cream!

Jellies, Jams, Butters, Leathers

Jelly is juice that has been made solid by the use of pectin, a naturally occurring rubbery substance that "sets" when pectin-destroying enzymes are destroyed by boiling the juice. Some juices—apple, plum, and gooseberry, for example—have abundant natural pectins in them to cause the jelling; others (cherry, strawberry, raspberry, and others) do not have enough pectin, and so pioneer women and traditional cooks added enough apple juice to strike the necessary level of pectin. Now, however, pectin can be purchased in most grocery stores and so there is no longer the disappointment of a day's work making jelly resulting only in a gooey mess. A general rule of thumb for the amount of sugar that must be added to juice for jelly is ¾ to one cup per cup of juice or fruit, but obviously that will vary with the kind of fruit—sweet grapes require less, sour gooseberries more. Too much sugar and your jelly will crystallize; too little will cause the stuff to ferment. Of course, jelly can be sealed in mason jars, but don't forget the old trick of sealing of jelly jars with a layer of melted paraffin poured over the top. I have no idea how effective this is, but think of the joy that a wad of paraffin with a bit of jelly residue on it brings to the child who can spend the rest of the day chewing the stuff.

Jam is crushed fruit or berries put through the same process as jelly but not strained, thus including the skins, pulp—all the good stuff. I prefer jams to jellies every time. Boil up your pulp, boiling it all until enough moisture is cooked off to make the goo stiff. Put it in a jar and seal. Mason jars with canning lids are nice but not nearly as much fun for kids as paraffin melted and poured over the top. Adding pectin will stiffen the mixture. By the way, you can check your pectin content by taking a small sample of the juice and dropping it into a teaspoon or two of methylated alcohol. Whatever pectin there is in the juice will solidify in ten or fifteen minutes and settle to the bottom of the container, giving you a rough idea of how much pectin is naturally available in the fruit.

Butters, it seems to me, offer the best possibilities for emergency foods because, while they require more time to prepare, they are also more condensed and ergo more effi-

Blow

I have no idea why elder flowers are called elder*blow*, but I do know these huge heads of creamy, intoxicatingly fragrant flowers are some of my favorites. I'm sure part of it is that I'm partial to those wild foods you don't have to pick away at for hours to get a teaspoon of nutrition. Elderberries yield up more than enough of fruit or flowers to make the little effort it takes to gather them worthwhile. Just bend the huge heads over your bucket or blanket and shake, comb with a coarse comb, or pull with loose fingers, and you will soon have all you need for elderberry wine or elderblow tea.

Elderblow tea is a bit too flowery for me, but a few flowers floated on a cup are really quite elegant and do add a very nice (when subtle) taste to pedestrian tea. Both the berries and blow are also a favorite to be mixed in with biscuit dough before baking, in the kitchen or a Dutch oven. I'm not sure either does much more than add interest and charm, but there is, after all, something to be said for interest and charm. Nothing fancy here: Just add flowers or berries, mix, and bake as usual. And then act like there's some kind of big secret to the process so everyone thinks you're a genius.

cient in terms of nutrition. Butters in this sense have nothing to do with dairy products of the same name. They are quite simply fruit and berry pulps that are boiled down and thus concentrated. The pulp, juice, and all is boiled until it is thick and brown. It may be nice to add sugar to the mixture, but there is usually enough pectin and natural sugars to solidify the concentrate without adding more.

I suppose it's worth mentioning here, too, that one way to obtain sugars in difficult situations is to boil down juices—grape, maple, box elder. Such things are now delicacies, although they were once necessities. Tapping maples is a lot of work, but as a hobby it becomes a lot of fun. You'll be amazed at the amount of sap that comes from a very small (three-eighth-inch) hole bored into a mature tree's trunk—gallons per day—and how little syrup or sugar it boils down to! But even a bit of boiling produces a sweet nectar, even if the sugar content isn't sufficient to prevent the syrup from spoiling.

Continuing down the path of cooking down fruits, berries, and juices, pulps can be spread thinly on a plate, tray, or even a board and dried to the point of becoming "leather," a term that describes the product quite nicely. Fruit and berry leathers are wonderful camping, hiking, or survival foods. When my interest in wild foods began, the only way to get fruit or berry leather was to make it; these days grocery store shelves are full of the stuff. Look in the candy or health food departments. It's not as good as the homemade—it never is—but it's passable. Here again, you can do this even with juices, or maple sap, and wind up with a chewy, sweet, and eventually hard candy.

Lovely Linda is an excellent cook. But as is the case in any kitchen, now and then things just don't work out as

Chokecherry Jelly

Wash and pick over the cherries, and put them in a pan with water almost to cover. Simmer until the cherries are very soft. Drain the juice through a jelly bag or layers of cheesecloth.

Chokecherries require the addition of pectin. It's easiest to use commercial pectins like Penjel or Certo and follow the directions given for chilly jelly, but for natural food enthusiasts a lighter-flavored jelly can be made by mixing chokecherry juice with apple juice, which is rich in pectin, adding ¾ to one cup of sugar for each cup of cherry juice and boiling the mixture rapidly until it "sheets" (runs in a sheet rather than drips) from a spoon. Pour the result into sterile jars and seal, cap, or freeze. Don't forget the paraffin cap for the kids to chew on.

Grape Jelly

Wash underripe to ripe grapes and place them in a kettle, ½ cup water for each quart of fruit. Cook until the grapes are soft. Strain through a jelly bag, allowing ¾ to one cup sugar for each cup of juice. Cook only four cups at a time, boiling rapidly until the jell sheets from the spoon. This can be sealed or frozen. To get more mileage out of the grapes, I sometimes run the cooked grapes through a food press and proceed as above, cooking until a smooth jam thickens. Stir often to avoid sticking.

Plum Jam

Cook washed fruit, strain it through a jelly bag, and put the fruit through a food mill. To three cups of pulp, add one cup of juice and three to four cups of sugar. Cook until thickened and smooth—about twenty minutes. Stir often. Place in hot sterile jars and seal or freeze.

planned. And here is where Linda lets me down: She calls her cooking failures *failures*. I keep telling her that smart cooks label fallen soufflés "Ouefs Bourdeaulaise" and serve them up with pride. A cherry pie impossibly sour because of a forgotten cup of sugar? "My famous Ohnezuckertorte!" best taken with real ice cream, of course. I get the feeling I'm not the first person to come up with this idea. I mean, come on—aren't the origins of Cajun "blackened" dishes fairly obvious? A derelict chef spent too much time with his nose in a brandy bottle and forgot to take the meat out of the oven. Solution? Pretend like you did it on purpose. And call it "blackened whatever." Say it with an accent and no one will know any better. Believe me.

This strategy is particularly important with jellies. When a jelly doesn't set, it is never, *never* a failed jelly. It is a particularly fine, meticulously prepared syrup. Put it on ice cream and you will be celebrated as a culinary genius. Curse, cry, and admit error, and you'll forever be the idiot who couldn't cook an elderberry.

Homemade Wine

Don't be put off by the homemade wine you have had in the past . . . the kind made out of Welch's Grape Juice by an elderly aunt in a coffee can sitting on her steam heat radiator, thick and sugary, as yeasty as a fresh slice of bread. No one who knows his way around wine will call that stuff wine. You get out of homemade wine exactly what you put into it. And even if you do everything right, there is still, always, a chance for things to go wrong and for you to wind up with nothing for your investment but something you have to sneak out of the house and pour down the storm sewer drain out by the street at night, a lookout ready to warn you if the EPA shows up. On the other hand, sometimes you take a few shortcuts, toss something together, and wind up with a treasure you drag out of your cellar bottle by bottle only for special occasions.

I don't have the room to give you a winemaking class here, but if you are at all serious, even casually serious, about making some wild grape or chokecherry wine, get yourself a good book on winemaking—there are hundreds of them. Or go to a good Web site and do some reading first. This is one place where I recommend you seek out printed, published, professional guidance rather than some old-timer in your neighborhood or Uncle Ralph, who mixes up his wine in a tin garbage can and filters the yeast out by sucking it up through a relatively clean handkerchief. Winemaking is a scientifically and technologically demanding process. While you don't have to become a professional, you really do need to make at least a nod to the right way of doing things. If you invest any effort or expense at all, you don't want it all just to go to waste. The first time you screw up and waste twenty pounds of beautiful wild grapes, you'll see the wisdom of this advice.

Use clean equipment and take precautions to avoid contamination from things like fruit flies. Use sugar sparingly and ferment in a cool cellar rather than warm furnace room. Use real wine yeast rather than bread yeast; you can get it from any winemaking shop or over the Web from a winemaker's supply dealer. If you invest in one piece of winemaking technology, make it a hydrometer, which will let you figure out how much alcohol you are going to get from your raw wine; that will let you be sure you have enough to preserve the wine in the bottle and yet, on the other hand, not wind up with a sickly sweet potion. Bottle your wine carefully. Drink it young; amateur wine does not generally age well.

Paradis

While boiling fruit and berries is an excellent way for extracting juices for drinking as juice or for making jellies or jams, you don't want to boil anything to be used for wine. A good part of the wonder of wine is the delicate esters— combinations of alcohol and acid—that create not only the distinctive taste of good wine but also the aroma. Some esters are so fragile, they don't even make it out of the crushing vat. The French use the word *paradis*, or "paradise," for an extremely volatile ester that is released the moment a grape is crushed. I had read about *paradis*, so once when a bunch of us were crushing tons of grapes in my backyard, we started sticking our heads into the vat into which the crushed fruit was falling. It was an incredible experience. There is nothing else quite so voluptuous—even obscene—as *paradis*. And yet it is an essence that doesn't make it into the bottle. Heating grapes, berries, or fruits pretty much spoils them for winemaking.

On the other hand, I have on several occasions found myself in a situation where I had an abundance of winemaking material but simply could not get it to surrender its juicy treasure. Once it was rhubarb. A friend and colleague offered me his large garden's surplus of the acidic stalks, an excellent base for a white wine not at all unlike a German Moselle—light, tart, refreshing. But how do you get juice out of rhubarb? I cut a mess of it up and put it in a huge press. As I applied substantial pressure, a few drops dribbled out of the spout. This clearly wasn't going to work. I didn't want all the cleaned and diced stalks to go to waste, so I decided to do what I could to save them for later use by freezing them. Later I pulled the rhubarb from the freezer and put it in the fermenting crock to thaw . . . to find that the juice flowed freely and generously from the thawing stalks. Aha! From then on, before using rhubarb for wine, I simply froze it and thawed it.

An even more serendipitous discovery came when an uncle called me one Friday from the produce distributor's

Gooseberries

Gooseberries make a lovely, light white wine. And around here, that term—*gooseberry*—refers only to the berry when green; once it turns dark blue or black, it becomes a "currant." In this area, central Nebraska, we have gone through a long, ugly spell when gooseberries have not done well. But when they do, I love to gather enough for at least one gooseberry pie a year. It's worth the time it takes to pick off the stem from one side and the flower remnants from the other. For gooseberry pie you'll need:

- 4 cups fresh berries, cleaned
- 1–1¼ cups sugar
- 1¼ cup flour
- 3 teaspoons quick tapioca
- 2 teaspoons lemon juice
- 1 teaspoon cinnamon (optional, or to taste)

Mix the ingredients lightly, put into a prepared pie shell, top with 1 teaspoon butter, let stand 15 minutes. Bake at 450° for 10 minutes, then 350° until the crust is golden—40 to 50 minutes. To test for safety and flavor, bring half pie to my place. Ice cream wouldn't hurt.

warehouse where he worked and asked if I could use some strawberries that weren't going to make it until Monday. I opined that, well, yeah, I guess I could use them. When I got to the loading docks, however, I was somewhat taken aback to find that yes, there were quite a few strawberries waiting for me—almost half a ton! I had never made strawberry wine, but I was always ready to give anything a try.

Again I filled my press bags with fruit and turned down the huge screw to apply pressure. And as was the case with the rhubarb, out dribbled a dozen drops. I couldn't freeze half a ton of strawberries, and these fruits were on the ragged edge of going bad anyway. So what now?

Bacchus looked down on me and smiled, that's what.

Do you know the difference between white wines and red wines? No, it's not white grapes and red grapes, which is what most people think. At least not always. White wine is made by crushing and pressing the grapes and fermenting the squoze juice without the stems, skins, and pips. Red wine, logically, is then made by crushing and fermenting the whole grapes—skins, pips, and stems—together. The processes of fermentation leech and release the color from the skins. And voilà! Red wine!

So it is not only possible but sometimes advisable to ferment not just the *juice* of the fruit but in fact the whole mess—skins, pits, flesh, and, yes, even the stems—together. I decided that was just about the only option left to me with all these strawberries: I threw the whole mess into a huge crock, added a good wine yeast, and hoped for the best. Which is exactly what I got. It was like magic—the fermentation began at once to separate the juice from the pulp. The pulp lifted above the juice as a cap, which I punched down into the juice a couple of times a day for a couple of days, then lifted the pulp out and suspended it in large cloth bags above another vat to drain. It was amazing—the pulp drained almost dry, and I was left with almost sixty gallons of fermenting strawberry juice! And then, strawberry wine.

I casked the wine in a huge oak barrel I had obtained used from a distillery and aged it for a few months. Every so often I cracked the bung to top off the barrel to avoid excessive air, which oxidizes wine and makes it undrinkable. And I very quickly discovered something magic. It is always a joy to open a huge barrel of wine and smell what's going on in the deep, dark interior. But I'd never smelled anything like the perfume coming off that sixty-gallon vat of strawberry wine. It was absolutely unbelievable. You had to be careful not to suck in too deep a draft because it would knock you out. Just the aroma was enchanting. In this case the essence of *paradis* did survive the press and vat and was still alive and intoxicating in the barrel.

Eventually I bottled that nectar, and though it was a short-lived wine—most wines improve for a while in the bottle, but not indefinitely—while it lasted this stuff became famous all over town with young swains because it was irresistibly aphrodisiacal. Not a woman in the world could resist a couple of glasses of this wine. Well, okay, there were a few *really* strong-willed Amazons who resisted its magic, but happy reports came from everywhere that a bottle of Welsch's Magical Strawberry Wine was worth its weight in chocolates, roses, fancy lobster suppers, movies about courtship and romance, talks about relationships, fuzzy teddy bear gifts, and even romantic walks along a moonlit lake.

Uh . . . where was I? Oh yeah . . . sometimes a good way to get juice out of berries is by freezing or fermenting on the fruit.

There are tricks for harvesting wild berries. Elderberries, for example, are like buckshot: small, and each on an individual stem even though they grow in huge heads. And they are thin skinned and easily squished. So how to pick them? Simple enough. Take a large basket or even a sheet, bend the huge heads over the container . . . and *comb them off with a large-toothed comb!* Isn't that clever?

Mulberries can be so messy, especially when they are at their best, full of juice and tender as eggshells. So how to pick them? Don't. Spread a sheet—an old sheet, because no matter how careful you are, that thing is going to be stained to the point of total uselessness as acceptable bed clothing unless it was purple to begin with—and just shake the bush gently. Mulberries will fall like the gentle rains from heaven! The tree or bush is above your reach? Spread the sheet and tap the branch gently with a pole. Don't worry about the berries that fall away from your sheet (and believe me, they will). Leave them on the ground to feed the birds and raccoons. At least those that don't wind up dyeing your knees to a permanent purple.

I once put up a hammock at a campsite and went off to do other things. When I came back it was after dark, and as I recall I'd had a few drinks with friends, so I wasn't particularly observant or careful on my return. That was okay, however, because I had made my bed in the hammock and it was ready for me even in the dark. I woke up in the morning looking up—ha!—into a mulberry tree full of ripe fruit. Well, great! I'll quickly have enough fruit for a cup of fresh breakfast juice!

But as I got out of the hammock, I had a new realization: All the previous day and through the night, mulberries had dropped into and collected in that hammock. And I had rolled around in the mash all night. I was deep purple from stem to stern, top to bottom. And I was that way for weeks to come. I told everyone it was part of an ancient indigenous tribal ritual. It was easier than explaining that I'm an idiot.

Sometimes a sharp, short knife, scissors, clippers—something to cut the stems—makes gathering easier. A basket or bucket is sometimes easier to throw loose fruit into; on the other hand, a cloth bag on a shoulder strap makes climbing and gathering easier. You'll have to experiment from picking season to picking season, fruit to fruit, what suits you best. My dogs prefer to stand on all fours munching away at grapes, sandcherries, or tomatoes within easy reach. I want to scold them but jeez, they seem to enjoy the fruit as much as I do, so why not give them a shot?

There are many such little tricks that you will learn on your own—or better yet pick up from veterans willing to teach them to you before you make all the mistakes on your own. For example, with gooseberries, pick the ones that are easily within reach without having to deal with the nasty thorns farther into the bush. Then gingerly lift up a big middle or lower branch and look under it. There you will find garlands of green or black pearls hanging well below the thorns, within easy reach. They are often the biggest ones—critters such as raccoons don't like to deal with the thorns, either. Prop up the branch with a stick or backpack and you can pick away with both hands. The worst way to pick gooseberries, it turns out, is from the top—where you are. God works in mysterious ways.

Indian friends have told me that if you don't approach chokecherries from downwind, they will be sour. I have approached chokecherries from upwind and they were sour, so once again the Indians must be right.

As in the case of mushrooms, you really do want to be sure you know what you're doing when gathering wild foods. I have never felt that a book is enough for identification; I like to have someone with me, a seasoned, knowledgeable guide I trust, who can tell me what plants are what, and if they are or aren't edible. Maybe it's because I have come too close on a couple of occasions. I once gathered a nice batch of beautiful, dark purple berries and had their wine already fermenting in my basement when a neighbor gently told me that, uh, well, he thought those were pokeberries . . . and, uh, while the shoots are considered delicacies as greens, ahem, well, er, the berries are rumored to be, uh, poison. As they indeed are.

You never know what the outcome of a mistake like that could be. My first book, *Treasury of Nebraska Pioneer Folklore* (University of Nebraska Press, 1966), had a recipe for the Danish treat rullepuls. It's a beef flank rolled with spices, soaked in a strong brine for a couple of weeks, then sliced thin and served on heavy rye bread or crackers. The publisher wanted to be sure the book was cleanly edited because the type was going to be set in England and there wasn't going to be much time to send the manuscript back and forth for consultation—this was long before e-mail. So editor after editor read the manuscript for errors, and I read it . . . oh, maybe fifteen times. And yet through all those readings, despite all that care, one potential typo made it through until the very last reading, just hours before the book was to go to print. Instead of directing the reader to soak the meat roll in a strong salt *brine*, a tiny little error had changed the recipe a bit. It said, by mistake, ". . . a strong salt *urine*." As an old friend of mine said upon hearing the story, "Wow . . . that might have spoiled the recipe."

Not to mention the disappointment and wasted effort. A friend once came to me with five or six five-gallon buckets of wild grapes he had just picked. He wanted me to see his triumph, and he wanted some advice on how to deal with the grapes. I went out to his van with him. It was very hard for me to break the news to him that he didn't have grapes in those buckets. Those purple fruits were Virginia creeper berries. Utterly useless. Not poisonous, but not edible, either. I tried to comfort him by pointing out that he had had a very nice day in the country and I didn't suppose the berries would do any damage to his compost pile.

Berries are the most obvious of the edibles and therefore the most popular with serious and occasional pickers alike. They can be picked and eaten without the harvester having to so much as slow down from full stride. And generally speaking they are the most easily identified of the edibles. Unlike most greens and a lot of roots, they are easily picked in lots and saved for later enjoyment by drying, freezing, or conversion into concentrated foodstuffs like jams, jellies, juices, and alcoholic potations.

One of the great stories in the history of agricultural marketing is that of farmers in remote areas of America, Scotland, Ireland, Scandinavia, the Balkans—just about everywhere, I suppose—who faced the harrowing task of planting a crop, caring for it to maturity, then harvesting it, only to have no way to get it across roadless wastes to a market where it could be sold. Okay, so the farmer could try to store that crop and eat it himself, or dole it out to neighbors before it molded and went bad, or he could load up his small wagon with corn or barley and struggle across rocks and through woods endless miles to sell the produce for a pittance . . . and then drive back for another load.

Or—or—he could run that crop through a fermentation barrel and a still and wind up with a few gallons of very valuable distillate that would keep forever and sell for a premium. Gosh, what a dilemma.

Of course governments figured this out very quickly and decided this same condensing of quality and crop would be the perfect bottleneck, so to speak, for taxing the bejeezus out of something that was not only economically ingenious but a lot of fun, too. And of course our enterprising farmer figured out that he could make more money by not paying the taxes on his illegal moonshine. And it simply added to the value of his product and increased the fun if he raised his middle finger toward the revenuers.

And an important source of fermentable sugars is—ta-da! —wild fruits and berries! The logic is not exactly obscure.

Not long ago I was in Bosnia to entertain some of our troops stationed there. One of my missions from long before I left for the Balkans was to find some of one of my favorite potables, slivovitz, a native drink made from plums. Or more precisely, to find some Kuralt Family slivovitz if at all possible.

See, my late friend Charles Kuralt of CBS once made a trip to his family's homeland in Slovenia, where he found (he told me later) that his family manufactured slivovitz, a favorite intoxicant of mine even then. He said he visited the family home and imbibed many a liter of his family's product, and I thought it would be fun to find a store that sold the same stuff, if that was possible in northern Bosnia, where I was about to visit.

It didn't take me long to figure out my misunderstanding of the situation. Every house, farm, shop, or store I went past during my visit had at least one carefully cultivated plum tree. And somewhere in the cellar or barn . . . a still. It turned out that, yes, Kuralt's family does make slivovitz. But so, too, does every family in the Balkans that isn't Muslim, and probably even some that are. Running a still is the sport of choice in the Balkans.

So I told my interpreter that I really wanted to find some good, local slivovitz to take home with me. Which was like wondering where I could find a plum bush in Nebraska. We simply stopped in the next little town at the tiny grocery store on the main (and only) intersection in town. Two young ladies were tending the business. My friend and interpreter explained to them what I wanted. They pointed

Cherrybim

Now, this is not exactly a survival technique for preserving wild foods, but I can imagine that if you have a stressful job in a corporation office somewhere, it might save your life some evening when you come home from work utterly fed up with the idiots you work with. A great way to preserve any cherries, domestic or wild, chokecherries or sandcherries, is what my family calls Cherrybim. Put a 2-inch layer of unpitted cherries in a large jar that can be closed tightly—any size. Then add 2 inches of cube sugar. (Granulated sugar has the annoying tendency to filter to the bottom too fast, and you want to keep the sugar up toward the top of the unit as much as you can.) Then another layer of cherries, then sugar, then cherries, and so forth, right on up to the top of the container. Then fill the jar up with cheap whiskey. You heard what I said. Trust me. Follow my directions.

Toss in a cinnamon stick or two, maybe some cloves. Over the years of doing this, you'll figure out what you like, and believe me, you'll be doing this for years. Tuck the jar away in the back of a closet somewhere and about Christmastime open it and pour off a little of the nectar. Amazing, no? The whiskey has been miraculously tamed and is like cherry nectar. Now eat a couple of the cherries. How about that? They have absorbed all the whiskey taste . . . what we have come to call "The Kiss of Fire." For a special treat, put some of those cherries on a bowl of real ice

> cream—not frozen yogurt or tofu or skim water/milk ice, but real ice cream. You have now officially tasted what is served every night after supper in heaven.
>
> I have recently tried cheap vodka in this recipe rather than whiskey and it is quite good although much lighter—maybe better for spring or autumn than deep winter.

to the shelves, where there was an obviously manufactured brand of slivovitz. No, I explained, I didn't want the commercial stuff. I was wondering if maybe there might not be something of local manufacture. Maybe from the several plum trees I could see flowering in the backyard of the store, which doubled as their home. They were uneasy. Don't Americans like industrially produced stuff? Why would this guy want some of their own humble product? Must be a mistake . . . But one of them went to a back door, down some dark stairs, and came back with a plain, corked, unlabeled bottle. She popped the cork and poured a bit into a little glass she kept under the counter. She handed it to me, wincing in preparation for what would almost certainly be rejection. I mean jeez, this wasn't the really good stuff pouring out of the big vats and pipes in the city factories; this was the plain old village stuff everyone there drank on Saturday nights! In fact, they pointed at the very tree behind their shop from which the plums for this batch had come.

And it was, as I knew it would be, pure nectar. I closed my eyes and imagined these very lovely maidens picking the

crop with their dainty hands the autumn before and crushing the fruit in a huge vat with their delicate feet, hoisting
their skirts up to their hips, dancing and singing local folk
songs as they worked. I sighed as I took another sip. I
beamed at the girls and nodded vigorously. I emptied the
glass, to their delight. They filled it back up. Wow, they must
have been thinking, an American who has come to Bosnia,
who has come to our small village, who knows about
slivovitz, and who actually likes *our* slivovitz! I probably
could have had sex with both of them right then and there,
they were so gleeful. But no, I left that thought, because you
can get sex anywhere, but only *here* could I get this slivovitz!

I told the interpreter to tell them yes, this is what I
wanted. They held up the bottle, asking (he told me) if I
wanted the whole bottle or just another couple of slugs. The
whole bottle? Good grief, no! I wanted six! They were astonished. This would, they said, deplete not just the family but
even the village supply. But, well, uh, there would be more
plums soon. And one of them went back down the stairs,
emerging with an armload of the magic bottles.

The interpreter groaned and quietly told me in English
that I had just made a huge mistake. Now that the girls knew
I liked their slivovitz and was buying it up by the tanker-
carload, they would hit me with a price commensurate with
my stupidity. He said I should brace myself, and he asked
them how much the six bottles would cost me. They thought
a moment, discussed the issue, and then, smiling, said
something in Bosniac. Again my companion groaned. He
turned to me and said yes, he had been right. The girls, as

gorgeous and innocent as they appeared (you cannot imagine the beauty of Bosnian women!), were heartless when it came to business deals. They had arrived at a price and didn't seem inclined to dicker. They were demanding . . . $36 for the six bottles. Big bottles. Liter bottles. Of incredibly wonderful slivovitz. Six dollars a bottle, or about the price of a beer in Chicago airport. I dug out the money and threw it at them, suppressing my hilarity and urging the interpreter to run with me back to our Humvee before these girls figured out that they had been, at least figuratively, screwed but good. I probably should have bargained for their fleshy affections, too. After all, I seemed to be having a run of real luck here.

The next step was getting six unlabeled bottles of clear, obviously volatile explosives through customs and back to my rural home, where I could bury it in my backyard or lock in a vault. God smiles on the pure of heart and the wondrous of imbibing, apparently, because the customs folks waved me right on through and I drove the two hours homeward, giggling insanely the whole way. To this day I am nursing along the remaining bottles of that wonderful stuff, halfway around the world from the plum trees where it was made and the lithesome, comely maidens who frolicked to make it.

The moral is, don't underestimate what apparently nontechnical societies can do with wild foods. They do have a technology. But it is a technology developed and transmitted over long, long times to a local taste, that taste simultaneously growing toward the virtues of the local growth and process. And another moral is, everything ferments. And don't forget—everyone makes alcohol, including beautiful young Bosnian girls.

And old German-Russian grandmas. My paternal grandmother would never have let the demon alcohol cross her lips. Except beer, of course, she being German and beer not really being alcohol in her estimation. And her "cough medicine," of course, which couldn't be considered alcohol since it was medicine. And since it was homemade. At least once each winter, Grandma took the huge iron pot in which she cooked for her family of nine and filled it with *Schnitz* (mixed dried fruit) and water, and with any sugar she might be able to find and spare. She put the lid on it and sat it behind the cookstove, where it could quietly "work" in the gentle warmth. She had no idea of the science behind what went on in that pot, but the yeast that covers any and all fruit went crazy in that warm, sweet environment, quickly converting any and all sugars into alcohol. After a week Gran took the big pot and put it on top of the warm-to-hot stove. She put a mason jar in the center of the pot, on a canning rack sitting right down in the fermented *Schnitz*. She replaced the lid, but this time *upside down*, the handle facing down right over the jar, the hollow top facing up. In the hollow of the inverted lid, she put snow.

As the mash in the pot heated, the alcohol evaporated . . . much sooner and faster than the water. And the alcohol recondensed on the cold iron lid, then ran down to the handle and dripped into the jar in the center of the pot. After a day or two of this process, that quart mason jar was filled with a clear liquid—Granny's cough medicine. When this magic elixir was mixed with a little fruit juice, it worked wonderfully, calming coughs and sending children into a comfortable, long sleep after which they recovered quickly. Sometimes they even asked for another dose of the medicine. Even when grown, her children came to her for treatment when they had a bad cough. Or felt a bad cough coming on. Or feared someone else might give them a cough. Sometime.

Even if you are not interested or able to make a major investment in berry picking and preserving, when you find something in season, it will quickly become a habit for you to pick just a few cups and carry them home or to the campsite to rinse off and toss into your evening's biscuit dough or morning's pancake batter. Just a touch of wild berry flavor adds a mountain of class to ordinary food, not to mention a good deal of nutrition, and worlds of color and interest. You don't need a recipe for that—pick, rinse, toss, mix, bake or griddle. Voilà! You're a prize cook!

Roseberries?

I don't know what to call rose hips. It doesn't do much good to call them "hips." What's a *hip*? Why not roseberries? Well, that's what rose hips are—roseberries. They are the small red fruit left on the bush when the flower is gone, and my experience here on America's Great Plains is that they have to be about the most common and visible wild food there is. And convenient! Wild grapes, gooseberries, plums—they don't hang around on the stem long after they are ripe. But rose hips can be seen vividly shining red-orange through the snows of deep winter.

Rose hips are pretty bland to be much prized, but I just found and bought a jar of rose hip jelly from Bosnia on a local grocer's shelf, so they must be gathering and using them somewhere in this world. They taste like a mushy apple, and I don't happen to like mushy apples. But they are superb emergency food because they are astronomically high in vitamin C, a crucial element of nutrition. Whenever I pass a bush loaded with rose hips, I always grab a few and munch them as I walk along, a form of preventive medicine, I guess. I have also had good luck gathering and mixing them in with pemmican, producing a dynamite survival or cold winter foodstuff. Hips have large pits and not a lot of flesh, so taking the seeds out of them can be a really tedious task. I eat them like sunflower seeds: Put a couple in my mouth, nibble off the flesh, spit out the pits . . .

Rose hips lend themselves well to drying and are often used in teas, again for their high dosages of vitamin C. (One caution: Be careful not to confuse the brilliant red-orange of rose hips with the same color of the fruit of the bitter-sweet vine. Rose hips grow on prickly rose*bushes*; bitter-sweet grows on vines.) In a survival situation, rose hips are very valuable because they dry naturally on the vine and survive well into the winter. And they are easily spotted even in snow. Tuck that information into your mental survival kit!

Hippie Gastronomy

One of the first things I ran into in my sojourns with the Omaha and Lakota was their traditional ways of preserving foods. While our pioneer forefathers were eating moldy fruit and maggoty pork, the Indians around them were eating yummies that have since become delicacies in the modern world. Look, Indians didn't have refrigerators, right? And precious little salt. And no canning jars. But they didn't often starve, either. So what did they do? They dried food. They dried strips of pumpkin and wove them into mats that were easily stored over a fire, in a storage pit, in leather bags hung in trees. They dried meat and it kept for years. They ate plums and grapes, rose hips and gooseberries that dried naturally on the stems or on village racks over a smoky fire to keep away bugs and other pests . . . like mice and children.

One of my favorite tricks from the larders of the Omaha Indians, my own adopted Native family, is to pound large quantities of sour chokecherries, make them into largish pancakes, and then dry them on a rock or log in the sun or on a rack over a smoky fire to keep away flies and other insects. Now, there is a problem here: Chokecherries are more pit than cherry. And what's more, the pits contain enough cyanic acid that they can be toxic to cows. But when dried, the volatile poison evaporates away. The black, dried berry pancakes were used during the long winters in Omaha earth lodges in soups, thus further cooking away the toxins and making removal of the broken pits easy. For many Americans a fruit soup may seem peculiar, but for Europeans it's a standard. I have eaten wonderful cherry soup in Finland, and in my own German-Russian home my mother made *Schnitzsupp'* out of dried fruit—peaches, raisins, prunes, and other fruits that were at the time cheap foodstuffs. Is fruit soup actually any good? You won't believe how good it is. And think of the vitamins that dried fruit brought to the Indian or peasant Russian household during the winter, precisely the time of the year when it was most needed!

Cut and Dried: *Wasna* and Pemmican

A lot of my buddies who are into wild foods, jerky, and that kind of food processing are enthusiastic about commercial dehydrators, available through just about any outdoor or sportsman's catalog or store. I have never gotten beyond hanging things by strings or wires in a screen porch or horizontally between two old window screens. I have, in fact, made two frames with new, clean screening that look like window screens but are better matched for a tighter fit to keep out insects. I put the one screen across a couple of sawhorses in a clean, dry area out of the wind; spread out the berries, leaves, nuts, or fruits that I want to dry; and put the other rack over the top. Given a warm, dryish day and a light breeze, whatever I'm working with is dry easily within one day. If not, I can turn the whole business over to allow the food to lie on its reverse side. The second day's drying is sure to do the job.

During tribal days, Native Americans turned much of their meat—usually bison or deer, of course—into jerky. They really did "jerk" the meat, pulling it off in strips, cutting at it with extremely sharp flint knives. The strips were then hung on racks over smudge fires—usually cottonwood in this area—to preserve the meat from insect infestations or the village dogs. Or the village children, who were also known to snitch a strip now and again. And as with today's jerky, or hams and bacon, the smoke also added a flavor we humans have come to favor.

But dried meat can be somewhat clumsy to pack away for storage or transport. So Indians often further processed it by pounding it into a powder known as *wasna*. (Meat is still prepared in this manner within some tribes for religious rituals or even household use, just because it's so darn good.) The powdered meat was then easy packed into rawhide pouches or ceramic pots and stored in the corners of earth lodges and tipis or in underground caches. Sometimes the dried meat powder was mixed with animal fat . . . usually bison on the Plains, skimmed from the top of soups or spooned out of large roasted bison bones as marrow. This was then pemmican.

Actually, pemmican usually had one more ingredient that made it even more nutritious than simply a high-protein, high-fat, high-energy food: dried fruit, perhaps rose hips, wild and pitted dried plums or grapes, or sand- or chokecherries.

Pemmican had a couple of advantages. For one thing, the fat sealed in the berries and meat. Even white pioneers sometimes preserved meat by "lard packing," cooking down meat, putting it into crocks or barrels, and then pouring melted fat over it until the container was airtight. The meat was then fished out of the fat as needed and remelted fat poured over the contents of the container again to reseal it.

Second, this mixture could be softened with heat and packed or poured into just about any available container. When a tribe, hunters, or a war party were headed out on an

Eskimo Ice Cream

If you know someone who has been north of the Arctic Circle, my favorite place on this earth, ask about about "Eskimo ice cream." That's what it's called even by Aleuts and Inuits. In fact, it was Inuits who introduced me to this delight in the villages of Qaanaaq and Sioropoluk, the northernmost human habitations on earth. In a climate like that, you need truly high-energy foods—like whale or walrus fat, which I also enjoyed with those wonderful people.

Essentially pemmican with a northern flair, Eskimo ice cream or *Akutaq* is nothing more than shortening (like Crisco) right out of the can, with some cooking oil (again like Crisco), warmed and beaten to a froth. Some berry juice or water, sugar, and whatever berries or fruits are available are then mixed in. There are no natural berries or fruits in Qaanaaq or Sioropoluk, but farther south where they can be found or where they are imported to markets, salmonberries, blueberries, lingonberries, raisins, prunes, or anything of that sort can be added. In northern Canada and Alaska, there are plenty of berries that are just perfect for *Akutaq*.

expedition, new moccasins were filled with pemmican and carried as provisions. The mixture could be eaten as it was, right from the container, or mixed in with soup or boiled with water as soup. And of course when the food was all gone, the "containers" were worn as footwear!

I make pemmican these days with raisins, rose hips, cranberries, or dried mixed fruit. I have been told that mulberries dry up nicely, growing flavor-enhanced in the process, and make an excellent addition to pemmican. I've never tried it, but I will next spring. I like game fats more than beef suet. In our home we eat more buffalo than anything else, and buffalo fat, especially bone marrow fat, makes incredibly good pemmican.

Don't judge pemmican by what it looks like, or tastes like, in the warmth and comfort of your kitchen. It's a high-energy, cold-weather food, and believe me, when you are freezing and really hungry while struggling on snowshoes or skis through waist-deep powder, trying to pitch a tent in a 50-mile-per-hour wind at 10,000 feet, it will taste perfectly wonderful.

I mix my pemmican in small plastic bags that can be carried safely and cleanly in a backpack without messing up other stuff in there. The contents can then be eaten directly from the bag or squeezed into a pot with whatever else you're having for a meal. Add some water to make a high-energy soup. A bit melted down and poured over wild greens is super!

Chapter Nine

THE ROOT OF
THE MATTER

 A weed is no more than a flower in disguise.

—James Russell Lowell

There is something special about edible roots. For one thing, they tend to be more substantial than seeds. Pigweed produces huge quantities of tiny black seeds that can be roasted and eaten in breads, but man, no matter how plentiful they are, they're still so small, it's hard to be impressed by them. But you dig up a couple of arrowhead or Jerusalem artichoke tubers, and you *have* something! Still, the big thing about roots is—you can't see them. It's like fishing—you can't see what's going on outside your vision. And then there is the mystery of a nibble, then a bite, and then . . . that bobber goes down and your heart pounds.

Same with roots. Above the ground there are clues that you see but most others you don't. They see just another patch of grass. Or if they belong to the Tabernacle of the

Bluegrass God, they see watergrass and instantly seethe with hatred. But you . . . *you* know that under those pale green leaves are nuggets of juicy, crisp, clean taste. And when you dig up those hidden treasures, everyone is amazed. And you are never left without some amazement yourself.

Jerusalem Artichokes

When it comes to being well fed, you want to be sure you know your way around arrowhead and cattails. They are nature's bounty, and that's for sure. But in the winter mucking around in water and mire loses some of the charm it has in August, or even September. When I want to stay dry and warm, my favorites are Jerusalem artichokes, which as many authors have pointed out are neither artichokes nor from Jerusalem. They look for all the world like puny sunflowers, but the leaves are shaped more like lance heads than huge hearts, and the flowers lack the dark, seeded center. For reasons maybe not even botanists know, the yellow petals around the dark center of the flower look like they have been tortured and distorted by some sort of death ray. They tend to be uneven around the edge, bent, and twisted. (It's worth noting that if you have a hard time identifying this yellow, center-with-yellow-petals kind of plant, you're not alone. Lady Bird Johnson referred to them delicately as "DYCs"—"damned yellow composites!" Driving along the roadside with Charles Kuralt, she once pointed to them and ID'ed them as DYCs. He had to ask. She answered him.)

The thumb-size and -shaped tubers under those

Jerusalem artichokes are excellent fare. Dig them in the fall when they are as large as they are going to get and have stored up all the energy they can. (You will also find these roots for sale commercially now and then in upscale grocery stores, but of course the domesticated varieties are much larger than the wild. If you find some, it would be a good idea to buy them, look them over carefully so you know what you're looking for, and then do some cooking to find out how you like them best, or if you like them at all. If harvesting weeds in the wild is fun, gathering them in the supermarket does have its advantages.)

A real consideration with Jerusalem artichokes is that even when other root plants are impossible to get at—perhaps because of frozen muck or ice, or because they are very difficult to locate once their growth has stopped and the tops above the surface of the ground have fallen away, or because the roots don't last beyond the autumn—they are available and good eating well after frost. One winter I had planted a patch of artichokes in our yard, and a blanket of snow kept the ground from freezing hard well into winter—through February. All winter long we dug and ate tubers from that patch. I made note of that in my thoughts about survival foods, you can be sure.

I have eaten Jerusalem artichokes raw and like them. They taste somewhat resinous, but then I'm a guy who likes Greek retsina wine that tastes for all the world like turpentine, so you may not want to trust me on this.

My children have always preferred this plant root boiled and served up like mashed potatoes, in which form it is creamier than potatoes, and tastier. My best successes have been boiling them in two changes of water until they are tender completely through to the fork. Then I peel off the thin shell of the tuber and enjoy the mushy, sweet, potato-like flesh. A little gravy or butter makes the dish truly elegant, but often with wild foods I like to eat the dish as is in order to get the full, pure impact of its natural flavor.

One curious thing I probably should warn you about when boiling up Jerusalem artichokes: The water you boil them in will turn green. And if you get it cool, it may jell, or "set up." Don't let these quirks put you off. You're not poisoning yourself. That's just the way Jerusalem artichokes are.

Nut Sedge

My favorite root edible—not so much for food value as for fun, novelty, and wonderful taste thrills—is nut sedge. Part of the attraction has always been my suburban neighbors (when I had such) wondering what the heck my children and I were doing out there digging in the lawn, squealing with glee, and then *eating* something when we certainly didn't show much interest in our lawn otherwise. This stuff is also known as chufa, knotgrass, or watergrass. The leaf blades are longer and wider than those of bluegrass but are pretty much the same shape. This stuff is a lighter green, however, and a bit yellowish. Once you know what nut grass is (it occasionally shows up in specialty sections of *really* progressive supermarkets as chufa), you'll never again miss it in a lawn, whether it's only one or two plants or, if you're *really* lucky, a huge patch! It likes low, moist ground (whence the name *watergrass*) and is common as crabgrass . . . a bane for bluegrass worshipers, a boon for foragers.

It is also called knotgrass or nut sedge because hidden underground, sometimes attached to the long, thin roots as much as a foot away, are—*nuts*! These little tubers are in my experience about the size of a smallish marble, but an air force survival book I once saw said that they can be as much as a full inch in diameter. I'm not sure I could emotionally handle finding something this yummy as big as an inch in diameter. They look something like shelled filberts.

You turn a small spade of dirt over under a nut sedge plant; you won't have to dig deep, because the roots run horizontally not far beneath the surface. The nuts are easy to spot and often fall clear of the dirt without any effort on your part.

For my family, nut sedge is a bit like asparagus: so good it's always eaten raw and never makes it to the cooking pots. We clean nut sedge by throwing it into a colander or sieve and washing it with lots of water, agitating the strainer to jar loose any dirt stuck in the slightly hairy husk. It rarely takes more than that. And then we just eat it. It's edible, husk and all. To me and my children, nut sedge has the definite taste of coconut. In fact, I can't tell the difference. But to my amazement, some other people I've asked to sample the nuts don't make that association at all—but nonetheless find the nuts crunchy and tasty.

The nuts can be boiled and eaten as a kind of tuberous vegetable, or ground and mixed with flour to be baked into coconut bread or, even better, coconut cookies.

Meadow Salsify

Meadow salsify, another favorite root weed of mine, is also known as yellow goatsbeard (because the inverted immature flower does kind of look like a yellow goat's beard if you squint a little) and oyster root or oyster plant, which is why this plant is of interest to us here. Even out here on the Great Plains, if you know your wild plants, you can enjoy a fresh seafood dinner. (Whenever I travel the 300 miles east to Des Moines on business or to see friends, I make a point of eating seafood, reasoning that I really should take advantage of being that much closer to the ocean.)

This is a good wild plant for the beginner because it is common and easily identified. It has flowers that look a bit like a dandelion, but much bigger. And when the seeds develop, they are just like a dandelion's "parachute" seeds, but again, much bigger. No kid grows up where there is a square yard left unpaved who hasn't encountered and had fun blowing the huge parachute seeds off a salsify head.

You are looking for a first-year plant—in the second year, the roots get large and woody. The young first-year plants have a single taproot and are flexible and tender.

I'm an inveterate storyteller, so for me, a plant (or anything else) is always more attractive if I have a good story about it. That's the case with salsify. I was once traveling England with an old friend, Jay Anderson. He is a well-known foods expert, and I had done some research in historical cookery myself, so we were making a point of eating well. Now, that doesn't mean fancy eating. Both Jay and I are attracted to peasant foods. We ate in lowly country pubs, we stopped at farmhouses and bought cheese and bread from the folks who were making them in their kitchens, we drank beer and cider in tiny breweries in minuscule towns where it was made.

But at some point we decided we needed to treat ourselves to an upscale meal, too, and Jay knew about a really fancy place with great ratings and an international reputation. So we dressed up insofar as either of us was capable and joined the tony set for the evening. When I opened the menu, I was stunned into silence—and not just by the prices, either! There under "Vegetable of the Day" was . . . *oyster plant*! Surely not meadow salsify! Not a common weed! Not in a fancy place like this!

So of course I ordered as one of my side dishes "oyster plant." Yep, it was common meadow salsify, in a wonderful white sauce, nicely presented, and absolutely delicious. Once again proving that just because you're eating weeds does not mean you are eating humble.

Dig up salsify roots when the plant is fully developed but before autumn, when they become somewhat woody. Dig first-year plants with a single taproot rather than a multi-legged, thick, hard underground network. Clean the roots thoroughly. Scrape or scrub them clean. I have not found it necessary to peel young roots because their skin is thin enough without paring. Steam or boil the roots until tender . . . and eat. You will definitely sense the pleasant taste of oysters. For this reason, if you are in a kitchen or have a complete camp setup, you can prepare salsify roots as you would oysters, with a white sauce. That's the way Jay Anderson and enjoyed them in England. Or in a stew or soup. Imagine being camped on a remote, clear stream in the Nebraska Sandhills, 200 miles in every direction from any community of more than 5,000 souls, hours from a supermarket, thousands of miles from the roar of the sea . . . and what do you cook up for your unsuspecting campmates out here in the Middle of Nowhere? *Oyster stew!*

Responsible Harvesting

When you pick grapes or plums, or even pluck shoots from cattails or poke, the plant quickly recovers. Not so with roots—you can do major damage to a plant when you harvest its roots. While some plants like cattail, arrowhead, Jerusalem artichokes, and nut sedge are actually *cultivated* by your harvesting, I am cautious and selective in my harvesting with root crops. While I can imagine, for example, digging up psorelea (also called tipsin, wild potatoes, or

Burdock

Another common meadow weed here on the Plains is burdock, a large, coarse plant with a heavy taproot its first year. And that taproot can be seen being sold at top prices in Oriental markets (I saw it in Denver) as "kobo." Like salsify, it is boiled and served with a sauce as a vegetable. And considered a delicacy. Call it a weed in the field, and a delicacy on the table. Seems fair enough to me.

wild turnips) or dotted gayfeather in a survival situation, I would not harvest these beautiful and relatively scarce plants casually, for the fun of it. I have transplanted gayfeather to my own land as a precaution should I ever need it for food and because it is a gorgeous plant (you will often find it included in flower arrangements from floral shops!), but we don't harvest it for food.

The river I am looking out on from my desk at this very moment, the Middle Loup River, used to be known to the local Indians as "Plenty Potatoes" because of the abundant population of *Psorelea esculenta*. But now there are none of those wonderful foodstuffs to be found anywhere near. If I did find any, I sure wouldn't dig it up and eat it!

The turnips are still gathered by some few Lakota to my north and tied into the artful braids you occasionally find for sale in shops specializing in Indian arts. And art those braids are! They are far too beautiful to be cut up and thrown into a stew pot, heaven knows. My Lakota brother Chuck Trimble remembers as a boy simply taking one or two bulbs from a braid of wild turnips hanging in his mother's kitchen and popping them into his mouth to be chewed on and enjoyed on the way to school. There are obviously some advantages to being raised in America's poorest population, South Dakota's Pine Ridge Lakota Reservation.

But as with peyote cactus, wild rice, and North Pacific whales, I feel the process of harvesting such rare and culturally central items falls only to the Native populations to whom they are sacred. We white folks have stolen quite enough; we can leave the Native peoples at least these few fragments of their world we haven't yet destroyed.

Chapter Ten
NUTS TO YOU

 The king of Spain's daughter came to visit me
And all for the sake of my little nut tree . . .

—Anonymous children's folk rhyme

Is there any nut in America (other than gun-nuts) more abundant than the acorn? I doubt it. About mid-September you can hardly drive through our small town park here in my little village of Dannebrog, Nebraska, without having your car pounded to a pulp by falling acorns. The squirrels are so fat, they are beyond gathering any more acorns even if their nests would hold any more. There are mounds, drifts, and piles of acorns. Half—maybe a third—of them have worms in them. And yet there are still more than enough whole and healthy acorns on the ground in this one acre of Plains land—not eastern woodlands, but *plains*!—to plant and forest most of America east of the Missouri River. Man, if those things were edible, we could feed the world without so much as shorting the squirrels one meal.

Wait a minute . . . maybe acorns *are* edible! Are they edible? Hmmm . . . squirrels, pigs, and turkeys *love* acorns. And what is this I read here? Well, I'll be darned: There were many North American Indian tribes that considered acorns a food staple, a major source of nutrition.

My bet is that there haven't been more than one or two kids in all of history who have opened at least one acorn and admired that beautiful white kernel so easily attained and not thought about eating it. I mean, jeez, to get a walnut meat you have to pound and hammer and pry and pick and you wind up with a few battered pieces scarcely worth the trouble, not to mention that even this is mixed with rock-hard pieces of hull. But that big, fleshy, ivory acorn kernel pops right out of the papery shell and is ready to pop into the mouth. And if I'm not mistaken, it looks all the world like a beautiful filbert! You look at that beautiful nut-meat and wonder if it tastes like a filbert. And so you pop it into your mouth.

And after three chews, spit back out. Acorns, as beautiful and inviting as they are, are inedible, too laden with tannic acids—the stuff used to tan hides—to get more than an inch or two past the human lips. And yet there has to be something there for the table. Squirrels love acorns, after all. And there's nothing a hog likes more than a forest floor covered with downed acorns. Turkeys eat acorns, so why can't *we* eat them?

Acorns and the Native Americans

Well, we can. In fact, as I noted, there were North American tribes for whom acorns were a staple. Even a prized delicacy. So what's the secret? Were those people that much different from us back then? Were the acorns different? What's the deal? Why could *they* eat them while *we* can't? Well, it's not so much *can't* as *don't*. We could eat acorns, and enjoy them. If we just knew what to do to make them edible and had the patience to go through the little bit of trouble to do so.

Like so many foods, it's all in knowing how to prepare them. And the secrets of making acorns palatable—even delicious—are not all that mysterious. There are in fact many Native people who still prize the oak nut and remember or continue traditional ways of preparing them. I am told (but have not seen myself) that acorn breadstuffs are still prepared, served, sold, and appreciated at some tribal powwows and other gatherings.

While working on this book, I decided that I would seize the next opportunity to harvest a mess of acorns myself and try various ways to prepare them. After all, not 300 yards from where I am sitting at this moment *Oak* Creek empties into the *Loup* River. That is an important connection, and scarcely a coincidence. The French word *loup* refers to the previous inhabitants of this Plains landscape, the Loup, or Wolf, Pawnee. And the Danish pioneers upon arriving here found a large—very large for the Plains—forest of white oak trees. There are no other oak tree colonies around here—not for 100 miles to the east. In fact, one of the principal characteristics of the High Plains here is the lack of trees, eliminated for millenna by fire and bison. So why is there an oak forestation here in this one bend of a small creek, isolated in a vast sea of grass?

Long ago a Lakota holy man, Richard Fool Bull, told me that such enclaves of plants well apart from larger areas of their more common distribution are not accidents. Native peoples planted and maintained such growths, not by tilling and working on a daily basis, but by deliberately carrying seeds, planting them, and continuing to plant them where they would best serve themselves and future generations. And of course then it was up to the white invaders to destroy those wonderful food sources deliberately or by neglect. And in the process tens of thousands of white settlers suffered and starved in an environment their Indian neighbors had always considered generous and bountiful to the extreme.

Well, fortunately some of the fine old white oaks along Oak Creek as it runs through my little town of Dannebrog, Nebraska, have survived the malignancy of white settlement. In fact, our small town park is canopied with huge old oaks. So this year in early September, I made a point of starting an acorn watch in the park. I took a bucket and rake at first and gathered what I could from the grassy lawn and gravelly road. I did okay, but it was a little clumsy and the acorns required more than a little sorting from the sticks, leaves, gum wrappers, and rocks I gathered along with them. A friendly neighbor came by one day while I was at my harvest task and suggested that, uh, maybe what I should do is go over there to the tennis/basketball court (he pointed to the concrete slab about 50 feet away) and simply shovel all the acorns I wanted into the back of my pickup truck. The situation for this acorn harvest was even better than his suggestion recommended: In order to clear the court for their games, kids had swept days' worth of acorns to the margins of the court. There were literally drifts of clean, dry acorns all around the perimeter of the concrete slab. What had been taking me a quarter hour before now took less than a minute.

I jokingly e-mailed my Lakota brother Chuck Trimble that I thought I had stumbled on the secret of how Native peoples had harvested the huge quantities of acorns it would have taken to nourish a clan or even tribe through long prairie winters: They simply raked them up off tennis and basketball courts. He explained that no, actually what the Lakota did was to let the squirrels eat the acorns . . . and then they ate the squirrels. I can always count on Chuck for solid historical and practical advice.

Most historical and contemporary accounts of preparing acorns for food do specify that white and burr oak are the best choices, because so-called black oak like the pin oak are much more bitter. You can easily determine what kind of oak you are dealing with by looking at the leaves: White oaks have nicely rounded, lobed leaves, while black oak leaves have pointy projections.

The Meat of the Matter

The next task was to open the acorns for their meats. On a sunny, warm afternoon I sat myself down on our patio porch and began sorting, cracking, and cleaning my harvest. I kept some mental notes of the process so I could pass them along here. I figured out pretty quickly that the acorns with small round holes in them were sure to have worms; that saved me the trouble of opening them and suffering the disappointment of another spoiled nutmeat. I soon learned, too, that there wasn't much profit in picking away at the bad parts of nutmeats in an effort to save what might still be good. A spoiled acorn is a spoiled acorn. The first batch I did worked out to about a cup of good meats per gallon of acorns fresh from the harvest. (Later batches were much more productive, yielding two to three cups per gallon of unopened acorns.)

While I sorted, opened, and picked, I wondered about the women who had done the same thing, probably on this same ground, centuries before. How did they feed large families, clans, entire tribes with such a slow, tedious operation? Well, I think there are many answers to this poser (as there usually are many answers to any poser, despite right-wing protestations to the contrary). First, the Pawnee women who gathered acorns from the same ground I did knew what they were doing. This is a common error of modern Americans—the notion that "primitive" people and processes are so basic, all you have to do to do them is to do them. I have watched Rotary Clubs and historical reenactors try to build replicas, for example, of pioneer sod houses, once so common here on the pioneer Plains. They buy or cut bluegrass sod with a modern sod-cutting machine, pile it up, put a roof on it, and call it a sod house. And it falls apart and collapses in the first rain. Then the new experts note and conclude how primitive the sod house was, how much the pioneers suffered, how little they knew about shelter, and take new pride in their own accomplishments in housing built of sticks.

They are, of course, dead wrong. The sod was different, to begin with. It was ancient sod that had never been cut — more woody root than dirt. It was native grasses, tough and wiry, not dainty and fragile new bluegrass growth. Pioneers cut it with a sod plow specifically designed to cut sod for construction: thick, solid, and undisturbed. Then the pioneers knew how to handle it, how to build walls with it, how to roof it and protect it. And as a result, the well-built sod house lasted for generations and provided solid, insulated, protective housing rather than "manufactured housing" that is gone with the first 60-mile-an-hour wind that sweeps in from the west.

The situation with things like working acorns is the same. We cannot judge the difficulties of such processes by the standards of our own ignorance. I was trying to relearn what I could about a process that tens of thousands of Indian women had perfected over hundreds of generations. I can't guess all the tricks they knew. No one can. But as a trained and experienced folklorist, I can tell you for damn sure that they had dozens of little tricks for knowing how to gather, shell, sort, clean, and prepare acorns that I couldn't come up with if I did nothing but work on the acorn-to-food problem for a lifetime.

For Better or Worms

Now, it's also possible that acorns they worked with were different. Maybe there were fewer worms in them in those days. Maybe acorn worms are a new phenomenon, or maybe just worst now than then. On the other hand, maybe there are fewer worms now than then. I don't know. But I suspect a more likely scenario. I can imagine my Theoretical Pawnee Acorn Harvester thinking, or even saying, "Aw, what the heck. What they don't know won't hurt them. I'm not going to get fussy and throw out every acorn that has a little hole or spot on it. It's going to be a long winter, and we need every bit of food we can get, blemish or not." (If that notion disgusts you, check out the FDA regulations regarding permissible levels of rat feces and insect parts in canned beans or coffee grounds.)

But in the end I'd be willing to put my money on yet another direction of culinary discretion. I imagine the following Pawnee village discussion between a child and her mother:

DANCING LEAF: *Mom, why are the White Cloud lodge's acorn soup and acorn cakes so much better than ours?*

DOWNY GRASS: *My daughter, I suspect it is because the White Clouds had all the luck this year. They got a worm in damn near every acorn they picked up. I sometimes think we must be cursed by the Thunderers. I don't think we managed a total of fifteen acorn worms in the whole lot we gathered this year. Sometimes I'm afraid I'm a failure as a cook. Acorn cakes and soup just don't have that special zing when there aren't any worms in the mix.*

DANCING LEAF: *Don't cry, Mommy. Maybe next year we'll be the lucky ones, and every acorn we open will have a worm in it.*

DOWNY GRASS: *You're a good child. Keep thinking positively and maybe the worm spirits will indeed smile on us.*

Community

But the most important single trick to the Native system of food gathering is something our own mainstream white culture used to know, too, but has somehow and sadly lost along the way—community. Sitting here on my patio, throwing out the wormy acorns, cracking open the ones that look good, throwing away the ones that fooled me, I managed to get about a cup of good meats per hour. Man, it would be pretty hard to feed a family at that rate.

Of course that's not the way Indians did this job. As I have said, for one thing they knew what they were doing. And for another, they might not have been quite as fussy as I am, or maybe even acorns were better back in the olden times (although that's just a guess). The big factor that I am missing, however, is that I was sitting there alone with my dogs, picking away at my bucket of acorns in dreary silence and solitude while the Pawnee women who gathered acorns from the same grove—maybe even the same trees in some cases—gathered in family, clan, and village groups, talking, laughing, gossiping, teaching . . . The secret of efficiency lies often in the community.

I look at farmers today, alone out there in closed tractors for long days, isolated, away from friends and family, and lament the new "efficiency." People used to do things together. Ten or fifteen families got together and harvested one family's crop, then moved on and did the next. How can that save time? It's the same number of fields, same number of hands, after all. Well, whatever the arithmetic logic of the situation might be, the fact is that many hands working together *is* faster, better, more efficient, more *fun* than working individually. Fifteen Pawnee women working separately, for whatever skills they had, would result in a far less final product than all fifteen of them working together.

As I cull, open, sort, and clean acorn meats, I think of things. And I wonder what lessons might have been taught during Pawnee harvest—

LIKE A MOUNTAIN: *Ladies, the acorns this year remind me of men: plenty of them around and they look good, but inside, a good half of them are rotten.*

RUNNING DEER: *Hey, Flaming Sky, I just opened an acorn that reminds me of your first husband . . . all hull!*

FLAMING SKY: *And this one reminds me of your brother-in-law . . . fat and plump but nothing but air inside!*

RUNNING DEER: *Daughter Yellow Flower, I see you are always reaching for the biggest acorns. Haven't you noticed that the biggest ones are the most likely to have worms in them? Sometimes it's the smaller ones that provide the most food. Look at your father—Skinny Dog. Everyone laughed when I turned down Rutting Buffalo and went instead to the lodge of Skinny Dog, but now it's Rutting Buffalo's family that begs for food while your father has never let us go hungry.*

[All the women nod at the wisdom of Running Deer's acorn lesson.]

FLAMING SKY: *Uh-oh . . . here come those three Sky Lodge boys. Yellow Flower, my bet is that they're coming over here not to help us old ladies but to impress you. Look at those boneheads strut! Ladies, let's put them to work!*

Other Tribes Heard From

I know women. I have three daughters and have had two wives. There's not a doubt in my mind that any session of acorn-working was inevitably visited by young studs hoping to impress the young ladies at the job. I imagine that the men were not all that helpful, because they didn't have the skills or patience to do the job right, but I'll bet that jobs were found for them to do that would show off their manly virtues while giving the women some help: carrying water, hauling away the acorn rubble, bringing in skins of more acorns . . .

All in all, you can bet that the hubbub and society of those acorn sessions went a lot better—and faster—than me sitting alone on the back patio with a five-gallon bucket, two dogs, and a pair of ChannelLock pliers.

In preparing for this passage of the book, I tried a dozen different ways of preserving and preparing acorns for food. I didn't go anywhere with that last idea of mine. Somehow there's just not that much Pawnee in me, I guess.

As always, your best bet when considering traditional knowledge is to go to the traditional bearers. My grandson Mark Awakuni-Swetland is a member of that venerable and honored tribe of the Wannabes; like me, he's a white boy who has found a home and soul among Native peoples, and again like me has been taken in by them and made a member of the family and tribe as if he had been born to it. The kind of generosity and love that is increasingly and so sadly missing from mainstream white culture is still, thank the gods, alive and well within the tribes. Mark has spent a lot of time among traditional people learning traditional ways, and like them he is generous with his information. I wrote to him about my interest in acorns, and he had a lot to tell me. I'll quote him generously during the rest of this conversation, and with my sincerest appreciation for his hard work, dedication, and generosity.

Here's what Mark had to say about gathering acorns and handling them in preparation for cooking when I told him about my discovery of the ease of gathering the nuts from the tennis court floor. I have done some editing, mostly shuffling of paragraphs and collating from a couple of different letters, to help Mark's good words fit in with my paragraph logic.

Dear Grandpa . . .

Acorns . . . Ate a lot of it in California at Yosemite. They had robust Black Oak groves in the valley of the Merced River. We picked the hell out of it for the Native demonstration program but also traded it over to the east side of the Sierras to the Mono Lake and Walker Lake Paiute at a rate of 100 pounds acorn to 10 pounds pine nut. I got spoiled eating it daily for 7 years. Got so I could taste the difference between our Black Oak and some Tan Bark Oak that came up from the Coast Miwok village at Kuhle Loklo north of the Bay Area. You're catching on about how to gather acorns.

The local Indians in Yosemite would wait until the custodians had swept the wide sidewalks of leaves and acorns into windrows then go scoop them up quickly.

We always spread out the freshly picked acorn in the sun for several days to get them good and dry before gunnysacking them and tossing them into the "chuka" (tradional Sierra Miwok granary). The modern day "chuka" is your old rez ride that sits on cement blocks in your front yard. Keeps the kids and squirrels out of the acorns. Put in a few bundles of wormwood (artemisia) and you can keep the bugs out, too.

Never did process fresh fallen acorn. Too wet. It would be 4–6 months old, at least. Multiple year old stuff was still good if you'd stored it properly.

Never ate the worms from acorns. They're full of tannic acid that you cannot leach out. Bitter!

East side of the Sierra Nevadas the Mono Lake Paiute would gather the heck out of a big catterpiller. About the size of a Vienna sausage. Roast them up and eat them like candy.

They'd also gather the fly larvae by the buckets full out of Mono Lake (salty water). Dry them out and crush them up. Looked black like pepper but as good as salt.

We'd gather the big white grubs that live inside the sugar pines in the high country. Kinda sticky, but full of sugar pine sap and sweet.

When I lived in Amatlan, Morelos, Mexico, we gathered a particular kind of small chapuline (grasshopper). It showed up in great numbers around February which *was fortunate because that is a lean winter time. We caught them and threw them onto a hot skillet and toasted them up. Took a lot of those buggers to fill a tortilla, but with a bit of salsa . . . not bad. The legs stayed crunchy.*

Can't think of any other tidbits to get your gastric juices flowing.

Preparing Acorns

The following section of this book requires some explanation. Over the last forty years I have eaten all the things I talk about in these pages. But to the point of the writing, I had yet to try acorns. Now, I can't put my finger on exactly why that would be. Maybe because of their reputation for being inedibly bitter. Maybe because there weren't many oak trees in the city where I lived. Maybe because the oaks I was familiar with were primarily pin oaks—a black oak with very bitter fruit.

I have a suspicion it was also because I had way too much information. I had read and heard about all the ways acorns could be prepared, all the processes necessary to remove the excess tannin, all the ways of cooking, and it seemed like a lot of trouble to go through. By this point you know me and my way of thinking: I am an eater, not a cook. I like stuff I can pick and eat as is, or maybe steam or boil quickly and throw onto a plate. But picking, sorting, shelling, soaking, rinsing, leaching, boiling, baking . . . oh, man!

So the day came when this book was pretty much wrapped up and ready to send to the publisher—except for

Cooking Acorns

In considering how to prepare "raw" acorns for human consumption, I had to consider a lot of historical and contemporary ideas. The main problem, obviously, is reducing the amount of tannic acid natural in the nuts. First, I wondered again if the nuts might not be a bit tart but nonetheless edible in a pinch. So I tried what the true scientist does: experimentation. But being no dummy, and not wanting to venture into animal testing, and knowing that squirrels and hogs do relish the nuts, I waited until Linda came walking by one day when I was processing the raw nuts and invited her to eat one. She took a nice, pretty, white nut meat from my bowl and chewed on it. I began the count: 1 . . . okay, 2 . . . still no reaction, 3 . . . a growing appearance of uncertainty around the corners of her mouth, 4 . . . a growing grimace, 4.3 open disgust, 4.4 unladylike spitting out of acorn goo.

Scientific conclusion: Raw acorns are not edible as is. They need processing.

I did a lot of reading, too, mostly in anthropological studies of tribes that ate acorns. I found a variety of treatments. The most common was washing them in running water over a sometimes substantial period of time—days and days. The Omahas soaked their macerated acorns in water with a mixture of wood ashes (preferably linden wood), which produced a gentle lye—

a base that neutralized the tannic acid. (If you are adverse to the notion of lye in your foodstuffs, do note that both hominy and Scandinavian lutefisk are processed with lye. It's not just an Indian thing, nor inherently dangerous when done right.) Baking or roasting is also cited as a method for reducing tannic bitterness, although I can't imagine how.

Again, here's what Grandson Mark wrote to me about his experience with tribal peoples:

> *Processing is* everything. *The ladies always had bits of acorn in various stages of preparation. Shell the dried nut. Sun dry the inner skin and peel off with a knife blade. Pour a handful of the acorn into a bedrock mortar hole (close-grained granite is best) and sit straddle-legged over the hole. Hole depths range from a mere depression to 12 inches deep. Use a 4–6 pound pestle stone of the same material and start crushing the acorn, raising the stone about shoulder height with each stroke. After a few strokes, toss in a couple more acorns. Continual pounding of a limited amount of acorn nuts will result in a mash. Adding a few acorn at a time tends to keep it as flour. After a short while the acorn will be mounding out of the top of the bedrock mortar hole. Scoop out the acorn material and spread onto a woven basketry tray. Decant the the larger pieces into a storage basket for later reduction. Upend the tray end, dump the finest flour that was captured between the sewing threads of the tray. This flour is mixed in a bit of*

water and poured into a wet packed sand basin situated near the stream. A small bundle of cedar boughs is laid on top of the flour so as to disperse the water that will be poured through the acorns. Repeated applications of water will leach out the tannic acid, turning the yellow flour a pearly white color. It will taste sweet. After all the water has drained into the underlying sand, lay the palm of the hand onto the acorn flour. It will lift cleanly off of the sand and can be transferred to a cooking basket for stone boiling.

Sounds easy, enit? So many specialized technologies and skills. Lots of shortcuts today. Grain mills for reducing the acorn. Laying the acorn flour over a muslin-draped screen set in the kitchen sink. Let the water trickle over it for a couple hours. Then boil, bake, or nuke it. I still like peeling off the baked acorn chips from the cooking rocks after they are pulled out of the cooking basket.

The young girls tended to be indifferent about making it, so it tended to come out bitter. Hmmm . . . Best Frybread: Best Acorn: Old Ladies . . . do we begin to see a pattern here?

the section on acorns. I spent a couple of weeks gathering acorns, as I have already described. And one day Linda was going to be out of town, and I decided that would be the perfect day to destroy her kitchen and see what I could do by way of making acorns palatable. I had read all the books, listened to all the Native resources, prepared an outline, lists, and a plan of attack, pretty much represented by the way I have organized the sidebar for cooking acorns.

But as so often happens with those best-laid plans, somewhere along the line something unexpected happened . . . and in this case it was a pleasant surprise indeed. As I ground, mashed, washed, baked, and boiled, I also tasted. And was very much surprised. The first option, acorns ground into a mush and cooked like a hot cereal, without rinsing at all, is . . . wow . . . not at all bad. At least as good as oatmeal. Hmmm . . . maybe I should try one of the ones baking in the oven . . . well! Also very good. Maybe Linda, daughter Joyce, and others had led me astray. Maybe acorns are good just as they are, raw and from the shell. I ate a couple. Not bad at all! And certainly not as bitter as I had feared and expected.

So what happened? For one thing, I do know that I had the advantage of working with acorns from white oaks, which have a reputation for being milder. And since I had gathered my nuts from an isolated enclave well away from the usual oak distribution, clearly an Indian cultured island on the prairies, is it possible the Natives would have deliberately planted acorns more palatable than the run-of-the-mill variety? Could be. Something certainly is going on here.

I also wonder about how much individual taste has to do with such things. Are my aged taste buds burned out from years of hot sauce, whiskey, lutefisk, strong coffee, and Cuban cigars? Could be.

Whatever the case, I found all the various ways I tried

acorns to be perfectly suitable for eating, and with very little effort I might add. If anything, far from being too bitter to be palatable, I found them bland. And then my grandson Mark's observation that the Omahas mixed acorns with black walnut meats made all the more sense: Black walnuts have a very strong flavor, which would work perfectly when mixed with the more bland acorns. I don't know that next fall I will go through a lot of effort to gather and process acorns for our household pantry, but I will never again turn up my nose at the notion of acorns as food—and you can bet

Acorn Eats

These are the ways I have personally tried to prepare acorns for eating:

- Finely ground acorn meal: raw, baked, or boiled as meal, like a hot breakfast cereal.
- Meal in water, ground, with baking soda to neutralize the tannic acid: raw, baked, or as a breakfast mush.
- Meal (rinsed copiously with plain springwater): raw or baked.
- Roasted whole.
- Boiled whole.
- Boiled whole and then roasted.

I can honestly say that I found acorns not just palatable but pleasant in each and every form, but my least favorites are the last three, roasted, boiled, and boiled and roasted.

I will tuck that information away in the back of my mind for use if there is ever a time when hunger threatens.

In order to experience the straight and honest taste of the nuts in each form, I added nothing except baking soda where indicated. I would think that any flavoring at all—salt, meat, flour, cornmeal, seeds (sunflowers, for example, or pigweed), other nuts (including nut sedge), seasonings, fat, berries, what have you—would go a long ways toward enhancing the blandness of acorns.

I can't imagine that we are going to be seeing Acorn Helper on our grocery store shelves very soon, but I know for darn sure that if I were ever in a survival situation and facing more than a week or two in the wilderness, one of the first things I would look for is an oak tree. Few wild foods are as abundant, as widespread, as nutritious, as easily identified, as easily prepared, or as tasty as acorns.

Wild Food Nuts

What about other wild nuts as foodstuffs? In my part of the country, there weren't a lot of trees and so there weren't a lot of nuts. Hackberries are decent munchies when black and ripe but with precious little meat per pit. Kentucky coffee bean trees and honey locusts are often passed off as potential edibles, but the recipes and preparations seem pretty strained and the final products are never praised as gourmet delights.

We do occasionally find the lone black walnut tree out here on the High Plains, but hulling and then opening black walnuts requires a major commitment of time and effort for very little product. I should also note that grandson Mark mentioned along the way the Omaha tribal tradition of mixing cornmeal with ground walnuts. I'm not sure you can make anything with walnuts that doesn't taste good—if you're willing to go through all that trouble.

Perhaps the most promising application of black walnuts is the reported use of ground-up black walnut hulls mushed up in water, which is then poured into a still or slow water to paralyze fish, which are then easily gathered. It is reported that fish thus stunned are not affected adversely for the table. I suspect this kind of fishing is against the law just about everywhere, but I think it's an interesting piece of information to tuck away in the back of the brain for use in the event of real emergencies, when it's a matter of survival and not poaching.

Chapter Eleven
BOTTOM'S UP!

**In a golden hour I cast to earth a seed.
Up there came a flower. The people said,
a weed.**

—George Meredith

I suppose one could argue that it's pretty silly to bother with brewing up a hot or cold drink while worrying about survival, or even when just out on a camping trip. But we humans do seem inclined to flavor our hot water in some way or another. I can see a clear rationale for caffeinated drink—a kick start for the morning—but what's the deal with *de*caf coffee then? Or herbal teas without caffeine to begin with? I'm not the one to be posing the question, because I like a flavored hot or cold drink as much as anyone; a hot ginger tea on a winter evening is really special. Around a campfire, nothing tastes better than a mint or bitter tea. Well, okay, nothing except maybe bourbon in a tin cup. But that is so ambrosial it doesn't even count. Maybe flavored drink is a comfort device. Fine with me! Bring it on!

I guess that if you're going to boil water to make sure it's safe to drink anyway, you might just as well flavor it pleasantly with something gathered around the campsite. And those tastes have been some of my favorite camp memories, I'll have to admit.

I like my tea strong. I prefer green tea, rolled tea—gunpowder tea, to be specific. And I use a generous dollop of leaves in the teapot. Not so with wild herbal teas. Maybe it's that the fresh leaves are stronger than the dried. Maybe wild teas, like greens and fruits, are just stronger flavored than domestic varieties. But whatever the case, I find that it doesn't take much more than one or two bruised leaves in a cup of hot water to make a strong enough flavor for my immoderate tastes, so start slowly. As always, the mints and teas in your area, or this year, or this time of year, may be stronger or weaker than you remember from your last experience with this same plant. This isn't McDonald's, after all; it's different every time.

While we're at it, whether you are using homemade, wild plant, camp coffee, or Folger's out of a vacuum-packed canister, please make coffee right. I despair when I see people who should know better screwing up a good dish. You don't have to be a cordon bleu chef to know that when you're broiling a steak, you don't flip it again and again until every scintilla of juiciness is lost. Grill it on one side until juices come up through the top, and then turn it and do the other side until again the juices come up through the top. Now you

This Round's on Me

Even a generous tot of good bourbon in a tin cup can be improved with a knowledge of wild plants: Next time you are setting up camp and the powerful, tingly, brain-clearing scent of wild spearmint or peppermint hits your nose, look around a little until you find the plant. And come campfire time after a good meal, pour your whiskey over a couple of bruised mint leaves in the cup. You've heard of mint julep; well, nothing sipped from iced glasses with the tony bluegrass crowd can beat whiskey in a tin cup with just a hint of mint!

Along this same line, say you are in a camp miles from anywhere. All you have by way of potations is a pint of cheap vodka. Someone says, "Man, wouldn't a good martini taste great about now instead of this cheap belly wash?" And you wander off without a word, returning to camp moments later, and pour everyone . . . a glass of delicate, polished gin as good as anything imported from Holland. "How did you do that?" they ask in astonishment, the young buxom blonde in the tight exercise outfit smiling at you fetchingly and lifting her glass to you in an obviously seductive toast. You smile and lift your glass to her, glancing quickly at your sleeping bag open and inviting under the huge juniper tree just beyond camp. She smiles . . . and nods.

Pretty exciting, huh? A wonderful adventure even? (I'm talking about the mystical gin.) Well, the secret is revealed in the last line of the paragraph above. The evergreen tree so common out here on the Plains that it is literally referred to as a pasture weed, the commonly labeled red cedar, is actually a juniper, which the Dutch call *genevre,* and from which they got the word *gin,* because it was the bluish berries from this tree they used to flavor the liquor invented there. It's a pretty simple process, actually. You pick a few of the dark berries that appear to be frosted from the juniper tree, bruise them simply by smashing them between your thumb and finger, and drop them into a bottle or glass of vodka (which is nothing more than a flavorless—by law—mixture of alcohol and water). Shake it about a minute or two and take the berries out. No doubt about it . . . you have turned vodka into gin. And a pretty good one at that.

have a medium-rare juicy steak instead of that shoe leather you've been turning out for years.

Same with coffee. If you boil coffee, it is by definition going to be bad coffee. Thus, a percolator that requires boiling the coffee can only produce . . . *bad coffee.* It won't even matter how good the grounds are that you put in the basket. You're boiling the coffee; it's bad coffee. Boil water. Take it off the heat. Put in a generous quantity of coffee grounds to taste—best freshly ground, but we're not being gourmets right now, just decent coffee makers—right down into the water. Stir in the grounds. Let it steep for a minute or two like a fine tea. Strain off the coffee. Delicious. See? I told you!

If you don't have a strainer, clean cloth, or paper filter, drop some eggshells into the coffee as it steeps. That is an old and revered technique for settling coffee grounds. It has something to do with ions. I don't know any more than that. I'm a coffee brewer, not a physicist. Thing is, it works.

They tell me that if you leave the coffee sitting on the grounds too long, it will get stronger but also more bitter, picking up more acids as it soaks. That has never bothered me. If you use a creamer in your coffee, it will neutralize the acids anyway. To some degree I suppose it's a matter of taste; to a large degree it's a matter of what you're used to.

Teatime

There is an abundance of plants that can and have tradition-ally been used as teas, or—as they are more properly called when they are herbal drinks—tisanes. I have freshened camp experiences with hot drinks made from catnip, spearmint and peppermint, sumac berries, and yarrow. I have never been attracted to the results enough to make the drink a household standard once I got home, but my camp compan-ions and I have always agreed that the drink was interesting and pleasant enough for an evening's quaff. Okay, there were a few who simply didn't like the taste but that could have been true of even the finest teas and certainly of my coffee. To this day, after twenty-five years of marriage, Linda and I each morning make our own pots of coffee . . . mine being real coffee, requiring two hands on the spoon to stir it, hers being a pallid brew of slightly brownish liquid, vaguely tinged with just a hint of coffee taste.

Oh—there is one tea I discovered in the wild that I do now and then brew up at home. I was once camped near Smith Falls on the south side of the Niobrara River in northern Nebraska when I spotted a patch of something viney on the other side that I couldn't quickly identify. I waded the stiff current and was rewarded with the find of a large batch of flowering wild hops, probably a patch of domestic hops some German or Swiss in the area had grown during home-steading years for the brewing of his own beer. I picked some of the resinous, fragrant green flowers (more like cones, actually) and carried them back across the river (along with a batch of watercress I found along the bank as I waded back into the river).

I brewed up a batch of hops tea, guaranteed by tradition to induce a deep sleep. The taste of hops will be instantly familiar to you as the undertaste of real beers, even Bud-weiser, but more specifically of brewpub ales or good Euro-pean beers. (Here I am trying to offer a subtle insult to American nonbeers, which is to say anything labeled "lite," but in particular the utterly flavorless products of Colorado mountains, if you catch my drift.) Beer with malt but with-out hops is insipidly heavy and cloying; the hops takes the edge off that heaviness and provides just the right bite—including, tradition says, the quality of beer that induces sleep. A nice light hops tea seems to do the same thing for me. Maybe it's just the warm water, maybe it's just the promise . . . but I do always seem to sleep better after a dose of hops, whether it's in a warm tea or a cool ale.

Chews

If you are simply in the wild and thirsty, what can you do for a drink? To keep the mouth moist, it may simply be a matter of having something to chew on, like chewing gum. The Plains Indians used cottonwood cotton to this effect, or the coagulated sap of the cedar tree or other evergreens often found in globs at the base of wounds in the tree's bark—the stuff from which amber eventually comes. A few red berries from the staghorn sumac popped into the mouth give a wonderful lemony taste and a relief from thirst.

Of course, berries actually provide real moisture for the system. A handful of juicy wild grapes may seem too tart to slake a thirst, but when mixed with bland but equally juicy elderberries or mulberries, they make a wonderful and instant trail refreshment. Especially mulberries. They tend to be a bit insipid—too little acid—to slake thirst satisfactorily; on the other hand, it's so easy to gather a couple of pounds of mulberries just by shaking a branch over a cloth that if you really need a drink, mulberries strike me as the way to go.

Same with elderberries: abundant but pretty bland. A few gooseberries, chokecherries, ground cherries, or wild grapes in the mix makes a truly grand drink, because those fruits tend to be overly acidic. The combination is a real treat, for survival or fun.

If it's just plain old water you crave, but either none is available or you can't trust the quality of what you find, there are sources for a refreshing sip or two nonetheless. Cutting a wild grapevine anytime from early spring to midsummer will give you a surprisingly substantial flow of clean, clear juice that has only the slightest, not unpleasant taste. Cutting a vine and placing a container under it when setting up a camp will provide a good supply of drink quicker than you might expect.

Tapping a maple may seen a bit too complicated for a survival situation, but I have passed through my own maple grove here on the farm and been startled by the amount of sap running naturally from broken or damaged branches or bruises or deer-scratchings on the trunks. Actual tapping of a tree—drilling a short distance into it, actually no farther than you can easily cut by turning the point of a knife into the bark—will produce a copious flow of sap, only slightly and very pleasantly sweet. (Don't forget, any kind of maple will do. It doesn't have to be a sugar maple. Silver maple, even box elder, a member of the maple family, will do.) Don't do excessive damage to any tree with too many or too substantial slashes, and don't kill it by completely encircling a trunk or branch with a cut.

You may wonder why I am so stuffy about nicking a maple tree but so blithe about whacking a grapevine. There are several reasons for my callousness. First, grapevines like to be whacked. They thrive with whacking. If you don't believe me, take a look sometime at how severely vines in a vineyard are cut back. Second, there are a lot of wild grapevines—at least around here—and not as many maple trees. Third, it's easy enough to get lots of sap from a three-eighth-inch hole bored in a maple tree, but not from a grapevine. I wouldn't suggest cutting off a grapevine without a second thought—I believe we should have reverence for whatever life we take to sustain our own—but there are degrees of damage, and I honestly believe that cutting off a grapevine is not as heinous a violation of the sanctity of life as killing a maple tree. Maybe it's just me, but that's the way I feel.

I have never had the patience or needed water badly enough, but documents tell us that Plains Indians gathered the sweet nectar of milkweed flowers for a refreshing drink by shaking the nectar-filled flowers over a container or open palm, or by gathering morning dew in the same way from large tree, shrub, and weed leaves. I've never found myself in such a fix, but I suppose if you're thirsty enough, you'll find the time and will be grateful for whatever moisture you can glean in such a way.

Chapter Twelve

AND WHEN ALL IS FED AND DONE

 I know a bank whereon the wild
thyme blows,
Where oxlips and the nodding violet
grows,
Quite overcanopied with luscious
woodbine,
With sweet musk-roses, and with
eglantine.
There sleeps Titania sometime of
the night,
Lulled in these flowers with dances
and delight.
And there the snake throws her
enameled skin,
Weed wide enough to wrap a fairy in . . .

—Shakespeare, *A Midsummer Night's Dream*

Here's how I look at all this: There's this guy walking along through the woods, picking berries, rejoicing at a basket full of morels, putting plums in his pocket, tying sprigs of wild spearmint to his pack for campfire tea, gathering a generous bounty of arrowhead tubers while he's skinny-dipping in a clean, clear river. And over here is his brother, buying seeds and sets, tilling the soil and sweating profusely, hoeing and cursing the weeds, fighting bugs and rabbits, fretting about the weather, watering and spraying, and then harvesting what little remains after all the woes and worries. I realize that I am flying directly into the face of a world of morality tales with this kind of thinking—you know, all that about the grasshopper and the ant. But if you look around this place of mine, you have to admit . . . the grasshoppers are doing okay.

The new moral I am proposing is not exactly obscure: God wants us to eat wild plants; he punishes gardeners for their insolence and ingratitude. At least that's what I tell Linda.

I have always had a hard time answering the question "Do you have a garden?" Well, yes, I guess you could say I have a garden. But not like you think. When I lived in a Climax Suburbia, I carried seeds from the forest and meadows to sprinkle around my house. I sank plastic garbage cans under my downspouts so I could keep wetland plants close at hand without having to travel an hour to the nearest still or running water. I dug up roots for food but saved a couple to replant in my, uh, garden. So, yeah, I guess you could say I had a garden. But you wouldn't recognize any of the plants in it. Or exactly where it was. Or why my neighbors were so hostile about my gardening notions.

Now I have a farm along a clean, beautiful river. My neighbors are mostly cows, and they don't complain about the spread of my "crops" (which is not to say country life is without its problems . . . see below!). While I do have a wide variety of naturally occurring plant life, I still scatter seeds I find elsewhere that I don't find here. It's like a well-run grocery store, ever changing, ever restocked. I'm a lucky guy. I still plant mints along our drives and walks to perfume the air as we brush past them. I have a little waterfall in the backyard with small tubs for arrowhead, cattail, and calamus because they are beautiful ornamentals, their edible qualities notwithstanding. We planted the gray-water outlet from our home with elderberries, calamus, and cattails not simply because they are pretty but also because they work to purify the water before it returns to the soil, where it waters our trees.

Wild or . . . ?

Actually, the tough part is deciding what is wild and what isn't. If you're looking for a line or definition, you're going to be disappointed—or misled—because there isn't one. Most of our "domesticated" plants and crops, after all, came from wild plants and can easily return. Corn is an exception since it has been a part of humanity for so long, there is no longer such a thing as "wild corn," and domestic corn just can't make it without its human partners. As I roam the woods, prairies, and wetlands here on my own ground along the Middle Loup River in central Nebraska, there are many plants I see that are clearly escaped domestics—plants that someone had planted as an ornamental or as a crop which have since gone feral. There are large beds of lilies of the valley—not native to this area, and I sure didn't plant them down there on a former river island now part of my bottom ground. Irises, lilacs, daylilies—wonderful to see down there, but I know I owe them to someone upstream who lost them. Hemp, Russian olives, mulberries, kochea—once planted on purpose to serve a purpose now forgotten, and now part and parcel of our Nebraska botany.

In our own river bottoms, I have found the huge, coarse fronds of horseradish. Now, I know that horseradish is not a "wild" plant you'd expect to find growing in the woods, pastures, and river bottoms here on the central Plains. This magic patch of mine is a feral plant, an escaped domestic. But it is horseradish nonetheless, and I am delighted to accept the gift. The tender young leaves are zesty in a salad, and of course the real reputation of horseradish resides in its roots and in the wonderful relish it makes when ground up and mixed with vinegar, mustard, or other condiments.

Seeds travel and are dropped from passing cars on the highway and from deer, coyotes, wolves, and mountain lions just passing through. As are the animals themselves. Our fauna inventory has changed dramatically over the last century and seems to be getting even more dynamic—in the last decade we have suddenly seen growing populations here at my farm of lions, wolves, eagles, turkeys, buzzards, and howling mice. (I am not joking, believe it or not. Look it up—*Onychomys leucogaster*—howling mice!) We didn't have possums a century ago, but we do now. Ten years ago we had no porcupines or armadillos, but they're now being spotted to everyone's astonishment, including biologists'. You can just imagine what is happening to our plant inventory!

Horseradish

Okay, to begin with, wild horseradish isn't really wild. Like a lot of "wild plants," any horseradish you find is likely to be an escaped domestic, a plant that just got away from some garden—maybe even 200 years ago—and now enjoys its freedom. If you should be camped somewhere or spot some along a road near your home, you are one lucky person: You're going to get something for nothing. Horseradish greens are delicious when young and tender, but of course the real joy of horseradish is its root, or "Mother Nature's Napalm." Horseradish gets larger and stronger in taste as the summer season progresses, but it can be dug and used as soon as pieces of the root are big enough to scrape and clean.

Scrape the roots clean and drop them into cold water to prevent the pulp from discoloring following contact with air. Drain and chop the roots; a blender is a fast way to do this, but any food processor will do. Use caution when working with horseradish. Stand upwind. I'm not kidding. You will quickly find that the slightest whiff of freshly ground horseradish will bring a strong grown man to his knees. To one quart of ground horseradish add ¼ cup of prepared mustard, two cups of vinegar, and one tablespoon of salt. Pack the well-blended combination in small jars and refrigerate.

I have brought some wild plants here and transplanted them: calamus, a Kentucky coffee bean tree and a white oak, two weeping mulberry ornamentals—a real favorite of mine and one of the most dramatic trees I know of. Are they really wild? Hey, I planted them here after all! Linda scattered the chicory out by the road, and I have brought up gayfeather bulbs and seeds from a sandbar at the river to our uplands, where they are more likely to survive and hopefully thrive.

Other plants have grown fewer over the years. We don't see much in the way of ground cherries or, thankfully, Canadian thistles anymore.

Or, sadly, bees. Well, bees weren't native in North America to begin with. Here on the Plains the Natives knew them as "white man's flies," colonizing ahead of the frontier 50 or 100 miles. And now you hardly ever see a bee tree—or a single bee working a dandelion flower, for that matter. What an effect that change must have on insect-pollinated plants! I have run across bee trees now and then over the years, however, and while I recognize that they might be valuable sources of nutrition in an emergency, I have also had enough experience keeping bees to know that even when they are smoked and gorge themselves with honey—on the presumption that the world is coming to an end, they are going to have to make a run for it, and they'd better take all the supplies they can before abandoning ship—there are still enough of them mad enough to make life miserable for a sissy like me. The best thing to do, unless you are truly starving, is to steer clear of bee colonies.

Taming the Wilds

And what the heck are we supposed to think about wild plants that are being converted to domesticated crops? In Nebraska there are now fields of chicory, milkweed, sunflowers, and Jerusalem artichokes—all weeds just a decade ago. As corn must have been at one time in the long-forgotten past.

There are some dangers in tinkering with nature. God only knows (literally!) what we are letting ourselves in for with genetic engineering of crops when they start escaping and altering our landscape. But then I think I've made it pretty clear that some of this is happening naturally whether we like it or not, what with critters and seeds hitchhiking on loads of hay coming up from Oklahoma, Christmas trees traveling through from Colorado, cactus loads moving to markets in Grand Island, Nebraska, and show horses being brought to rodeos in South Dakota. Nature does to some extent govern such things on her own. It's unlikely that the armadillos, piranhas, and scorpions now showing up occasionally in Nebraska are going to change quickly enough to make it through one of our typical central Plains winters.

There are also problems with manipulating botany. Or trying to manipulate botany. When I lived in a city, I once cleaned some chicory on my front steps so I could roast the roots for coffee; henceforth my front yard was a blue explosion of chicory flowers. On the other hand, when we moved out here to the farm, we tried to get chicory to grow in our road ditch . . . like it does at our neighbor's place just across the river. We have struggled for almost ten years and now, *finally*, after a lot of work hauling seeds and trying to trans-

Designer Genes

I have always been interested in turtles. They are remarkable creatures, surviving as they do from the age of dinosaurs. A friend of mine once came to me full of excitement, thinking that he had found a petrified human brain recently dredged up from a nearby sandpit. He brought it to me from his car, and I recognized immediately that it was actually a petrified turtle. Even more astonishing to me, I could recognize that it was a petrified Blandings turtle. The Blandings had been roaming around here during the Pleistocene era, the ice ages, even before!— long before we humans were around to give them the name. Wow.

I was once given a Blandings turtle by an owner who tired of him and wanted to be rid of him. I was always ready to give a home to an orphan turtle. But eventually I moved out of my Lincoln home to my farm 125 miles west. I had seen Blandings here on this very land, so I was confident that my old friend would probably do just fine, but there is always the question: In introducing a new turtle to this environment, am I also injecting a possible genetic problem into the population? Perhaps a gene from a southern population that isn't equipped to handle the winters here and thereby dooming the entire species here to eventual eradication?

plant the stuff, we are getting chicory to grow on its own. Chicory obviously doesn't like being told what to do.

I planted calamus in our pond and it has done well, but there was also a five-year war trying to convince a neighbor to keep his cattle off my land, and out of my pond and calamus, a dispute that was finally resolved only after a lawsuit. A lunatic neighbor has ventured onto our ground with a backpack sprayer to kill our stand of staghorn sumac, insisting that he is only protecting us all from poison sumac, which doesn't grow anywhere near here. A demonstration of me drinking *Rhus* juice made from staghorn sumac berries hasn't convinced him of anything but the fact that I am protected by demons.

Subterranean Surprises

One of my best lessons in the hazards of manipulating nature came the summer I decided to transplant (1) some poke plants, and (2) a buffalo gourd plant to my backyard. The process seemed to be easy enough: Dig up the roots, dig a hole in my backyard, replant the roots. I started with the poke. The "weed" was growing on a campus where I was teaching, and the grounds folks were glad to have me volunteer to remove a plant that was not within their planting scheme. I showed up one Saturday morning with a shovel and figured I'd dig out the root, take it home, plant it, and then spend the rest of the morning drinking coffee and reading the paper. That evening at about six o'clock I finally managed to wrench loose one root that was, no kidding, not much smaller than me—and I am not a small fellow. Lesson learned: Poke shoots are delicious and about the size of a carrot. The roots are about the size of a Volkswagen.

I have never again tried to move a poke plant. They are quite fine exactly where they are. That information did not instantly transfer, however, to the much better piece of information of being cautious about moving *any* wild plant without some previous research. My next exercise in education was a decision to move a buffalo gourd plant. The buffalo gourd is a not particularly useful plant in terms of food, which grows in the western part of my state. It is interesting as a native plant, used sometimes by Indians as a soap. And the fruit is an interesting wild gourd. I thought it would be great to have one in my yard. So I went down a country road in the ranch country of western Nebraska and found a suitable plant growing in a waste area of a right-of-way. I was clearly not going to damage anything or anyone if I quickly dug up this root and carried it back home.

"Quickly" was not to happen. Not long thereafter I was at our state fair and visited an exhibit of native weeds. They had a buffalo gourd root on display. I wish I had seen it before I started digging along that country road. It was like that poke root I told you about. It was absolutely huge . . . as big as me. And I'm big. Take it from me and save yourself some trouble: You don't want to dig up poke, buffalo gourd, or morning glory roots. Morning glory roots? It's another story—and yet the same story. Just trust me. You don't want a wild morning glory root.

We have had better luck transplanting yucca roots from the wild to our farm. It took some time to establish itself, but now we enjoy the spikes of ivory flowers every spring. Yucca roots have been widely used as a soap, by both Indians and whites. They have a wonderful scent and suds up satisfactorily. In fact, if you nose around a toiletries section in a grocery or general store, I'm betting you'll find a shampoo that boasts a yucca scent.

I have dug up yucca roots to experiment with them in soap, and the results were excellent. But I'm reluctant to dig up such a beautiful plant just to wash my hands. It doesn't seem like a fair trade-off. Still, yucca tends to grow in wasteland washes and gulleys around here; it isn't at all hard to walk a wash and find yucca roots exposed, and maybe even a whole plant washed free from the soil, lying on the surface. In that case, I don't feel quite so bad. In fact, what I have done is to harvest enough root for household use and then replant the plant, giving it a better chance for survival than it had before I ran into it.

You don't have to do a thing to yucca by way of processing to use it as a soap except gather a small length of it, break it open with a rock, pull away the dark brown bark, and use the white fibers inside as a washcloth pretreated with an excellent soap.

Plants to Leave Planted

While we're talking about precautions, there are other things legal and spiritual to be aware of whilst cruising the shopping aisles of the wild. Nothing is nuttier than various attempts in this area to eradicate wild hemp—marijuana. I have in my library plant identification books that list hemp right alongside death camas and hemlock as a dangerous, poisonous plant. What utter nonsense!

Brainless zealots occasionally take teams of youngsters out to the countryside, armed with machetes, to chop down Christmas-tree-size marijuana plants in a well-traveled road ditch. You might just as well try to sweep back the sea with a broom—this Plains countryside is forested with hemp, an escaped domestic fiber crop of a century ago. Never mind that "ditch weed" (as it is fondly known) is virtually worthless as a bong filler (they tell me). Never mind that you could send every kid in our state out with full-blown flamethrowers all summer long and not dent the annual crop. Never mind that the principal result of such exercises is that children are taught *exactly* what marijuana looks like . . . probably the only wild plant they'll ever learn to identify, but certainly the first.

While hemp is often harvested in this area late at night for recreational use and nettles are picked as an edible green, neither is worth the trouble to my mind. My dear friend Kay Young, infinitely wiser about such things than I am, praises nettles as a green and notes that the nasty, painful prickles they cause when they are even lightly brushed against may seem to mitigate against their place on a dinner plate. In cooking, however, the tiny razor-cut needles dissolve harmlessly and become a part of the nutritional value of the plant.

Many plants are useful not simply for food but for other applications. In the case of hemp and nettles, it's the tough fibers in their mature stems that are worth keeping in mind. The poet Campbell wrote, "In Scotland I have eaten nettles,

Hemp for Fiber

Hemp and nettles have a long history as a source for useful fibers, for everything from clothing to rope. If you were ever in a pinch and really needed to turn to this expedient source, you might as well know a little bit about the process. If you try to pull apart a hemp or nettle stem, you will very quickly come to realize that there are indeed very strong fibers in there. But how do you get them out? How do you separate the soft green plant flesh from the stiff fibers within it?

If you are a crossword puzzle fan like I am, you know the word for "to soak" is *ret*. And that's what you do: You "ret" the plant stems, soaking them, preferably in running water, until the softer parts goo up, rot, and wash away, leaving—ta-da!—the fibers! Which you can then weave or twist or braid into whatever your heart (or your survival) desires.

I have slept in nettle sheets, and I have dined off a nettle tablecloth. The young and tender nettle is an excellent potherb. The stalks of the old nettles are as good as flax for making cloth. I have heard my mother say that she thought nettle-cloth more durable than any other species of linen."

There are other plants in the wild that are best left in the wild, whether the drawbacks be legal, medical, or even spiritual. The peyote cactus grows wild in the Southwest; I don't know if it's a cultivated crop anywhere. It is best left alone. That it is illegal doesn't bother me. Most drug laws are pretty dumb. But from what I know of the plant, it's an extraordinarily slow-growing cactus. I have watched one over the last forty years and it has grown from the size of a quarter to the size of a Cherry Bing candy bar. The question this brings to my mind is: So how long did it grow to become quarter size? Eating one of these cacti for recreation would seem to me to be like cutting down a giant sequoia tree just to hear the noise it makes when it falls. The peyote cactus is used sparingly and reverently in Native American worship, and while I am even troubled by what this might be doing to the cactus population, that at least strikes me as a serious and respectful use of the plant. No white man or even Indian should pick a peyote cactus. Besides, it's illegal. And it should be.

Honoring the Sacred

Peyote grows nowhere around here. On the other hand, jimsonweed or locoweed—common names around here for the datura plant—is common. It's a large-leafed plant with beautiful, white, trumpet flowers. I have seen it as a 6- to 8-foot-high nuisance in a nearby horse pasture and cultivated as an ornamental at a suburban curbside and in the front yard of a small restaurant. It is just fine in the wild or flower box (although potentially dangerous to grazing animals, as the name implies). But unfortunately some wacky people have come to the conclusion that ingesting small amounts of the seeds might be an interesting experiment or recreational adventure. And then they die, and it doesn't seem like nearly as much fun.

Again, some plants like peyote and datura have a role in ancient, traditional, recognized Native religious processes. The Indians know what they are doing and are sanctioned by the law and by God to use the plants. The rest of us are not, and there are good reasons for that. There are too many other ways to have a good time to take these risks. Not least of all, I believe we owe enough respect to those peoples who see some plants as sacred that we should consider their sacred plants hands-off for us.

On the other hand, some sacred plants *are* available to us uninitiated. Like my next-to-favorite tree, the cottonwood. (As I have noted elsewhere, my favorite tree is the weeping mulberry—but insofar as I am aware, it isn't sacred to anyone but me.) The Lakota consider the cottonwood a divine gift. It is a preferred wood for fires in tipis because it doesn't throw sparks, a serious consideration when you have a family sleeping around the fire wrapped in fur bedding. The leaves are seen as Wakantonka's pattern for both the moccasin and the tipi cover. To this day it is a cottonwood pole that stands as the center for the sacred Lakota sun dance. I love cottonwood for the song it makes outside my bedroom window in even the lightest Plains breeze. To me they are as much living spirits as Tolkien's Ents. When some right-wing fruitcake tries to insult me by calling me a "tree-hugger," there's not a single argument I can put up because for all I know, he might indeed have seen me hugging a tree, more than likely a cottonwood.

White cedar (also called flat cedar because it has flat needles rather than round, prickly ones like red cedar) is sacred to many Native peoples, its dried needles being used as an incense and purifier in all manner of sacred ceremonies from blessings to prayer and purification. Domesticated tobacco is used in the same way, but you'll sometimes encounter wild tobacco, red willow bark, or sumac bark used for the same purposes. Dried sweet grass and white sage are used for smoke in ceremonies, as well as for sachets for their natural perfume.

A decided advantage to using wild plants as domestic plantings is that they are *wild*. They deal well with your climate and soil because that's where they are at home. Hell, they know more about your geography than you do, if you think about it! I enjoy the incredible perfume of chokecherries and wild plums coming through my bedroom window in the spring. Then as I am puttering around, sometimes as I pass by on a tractor and simply reach out and grab, I get a wonderful mouthful of sweet, full, natural juice and nutrition. And when the fruit falls to the ground, I note that it disappears almost instantly as the real tenants of this landscape gobble it up—bunnies, possums, coons, turkeys, deer . . . So far as I can tell, nothing that hits the ground around here goes to waste except my own footsteps.

While I have concentrated in these pages on uses of wild plants for food, I have hinted broadly at other uses, some at least as valuable to keep in mind. An enormous percentage of our pharmacopoeia—our scientific drug inventory—has come to us from traditional uses for plants. And wisely, the

Something in the Air

Speaking of which . . . It's a long way from survival to spiffy smells, but I suppose that even as a male of the species (Linda says actually we are a totally different species) I can speak of lovely smells without being kicked out of the fraternity. And the truth is, I like wild plant smells. I have some braids of sweet grass near my closet door, and I love the slight whiff of the wild I get from them as I'm dressing for the day. I keep bundles of sage above our house doors both as decoration and for the cleansing and protective qualities my Indian friends attribute to the plant. Calamus leaves were spread on floors by our Pilgrim fathers for the scent they added to the air—and the ones emanating from the household's inhabitants that they covered up—but the smell is a little too strong and pungent for me. (The calamus, not the inhabitants.) The scent of wild hops was believed by some to carry with it the sleep-inducing character the plant imparts to beer, and so pillows were stuffed with hops flowers, especially in monasteries, where monks apparently had even more thoughts disturbing their sleep than those of us who have not taken vows of chastity. The flowers of elderberries—elderblow—are dried and kept as a sachet, and of course any mint, from fine spearmint or peppermint to coarse catnip, makes a refreshing sachet. Ask your cat if you don't believe me. And as I have mentioned elsewhere in these

> pages, I transplant mints to the walks and drive of my home as a living sachet to perfume my every step as I walk about—for example, on my way back to the house from the privy.

world's medical systems still look to traditional plant uses for potential new medicines. Dosages are so uncertain, we prefer these days to use commercially prepared and perhaps artificially manufactured versions, but perhaps it can still be useful to know that chewing on a willow stick is good for a headache.

Some peripheral plant uses fall within the category of practical application. The small worms found in the swollen stems of the goldenrod make a fast and easy fish bait, for instance, or if you are really desperate, the liquid from crushing and soaking walnut hulls can be used as a fish stun in a small pond or backwater, rendering fish helpless but leaving them still edible.

Sometimes plants are useful to us in totally passive ways that are scarcely noticeable within the normal course of our lives. Our entire farm and our house enjoy the shelter of thick juniper thickets that not only buffer the wind and trap winter snows but also screen us from neighbors and passersby and deaden the roar of speeding half-wits and the throbbing sound systems of adolescents who can't otherwise get any attention to a low whisper. All around us out here on the windswept Great American Desert, we watch people drag

The Dentist Botanical

I was once on a canoe trip on a river well out of reach of easy contact with civilization. A member of our party of lawyers broke a tooth and was in real pain. I don't know a lot about medicinal applications of wild plants, but I did recall that prickly ash was called the "toothache plant" by some Plains tribes for its alleged ability to deaden tooth pain. As it happened—and as it so often seems to happen— there, smack in the middle of our camp was a prickly ash shrub. And although I wasn't real familiar with the plant, I did recognize it. I mentioned its reputation, and our friend who was in pain said he would try anything at all that might help. I decided that feeding lawyers wild plants without knowing the possible effects was not the smartest thing I could do in this life, so I picked some of the berries, threw them into my mouth, and sucked on them a bit to see if there were any adverse effects. I was astonished to find that my mouth very quickly became numb. I felt fine otherwise, but no doubt about it, my mouth had been numbed by the plant. My friend did the same and was very much relieved through the evening and night. He carried some of the small woody berries with him for use the next day until we ended our trip and he could get real help. The wisdom of the ancients is not to be scorned.

in double-wide factory houses and set them on a concrete-block foundation—and never once in the first ten or twenty years plant a tree to shelter their tin shed from the wind, sun, and snow. My guess is that they are too busy complaining about the price of electricity and fuel to cool and heat the place to take the hour to plant a tree or two. I don't even know where to start with farmers who push down fifty-year-old windbreaks and shelter belts to plant another acre of corn we don't need and they can't get a decent price for. Then they complain about how the snows just don't stick like they used to and provide subsurface water. And their cattle seem to be so stressed by wind, heat, and storms that they just don't put on weight. Gosh . . . wonder why that is?

Rock-a-Bye Babies

A buddy and I were once stranded far from reach of civilization on a river island late in the day in a pouring rain. We did not look forward to setting up a tent and getting even wetter, but upon pulling ashore we spotted a huge, ancient juniper (here on the Plains often referred to as a red cedar), spared for over a century from sweeping Plains fires by the water of the river around us. We found under that tree a large, dry space, nicely cushioned by decades of fallen needles. We were amazed to find that the rain poured down and out as it fell through the tree's tall growth, yet not a drop fell within 10 feet of the gnarled trunk. We didn't even need to set up a tent that night. We slept dry and comfy in the bosom of that beautiful old tree.

Some uses of wild plants are blithe: A local dowser

insists that the very best forks for seeking underground watercourses are hackberry. He doesn't know why, and neither do I. It's a given in the saunas of Finland, where the sauna was invented (at least that's what the Finns say!), that before taking the steam one ventures into the nearby woods to gather, or goes to the local market to buy, a bunch of tender young birch twigs to use as a fan and flail to cool the skin and fan the face. And it has to be birch. Don't ask why. I don't know and neither do the Finns. Toss a couple of hedge apples from a hedgerow of Osage orange trees under your porch or shed and your days of worrying about bugs are over. (But don't try to cut yourself a couple of cords of firewood from that old neglected hedgerow! Osage orange is also called bois d'arc or bow wood because the stuff is ferociously hard, tough, and springy. You might just as well try to cut up scrap iron with your chain saw. I have been told it will actually throw sparks from a saw chain! I know for certain it will dull a blade or chain in a matter of minutes. Old-timers have told me that a fence post made of Osage orange will outlast six or eight postholes.)

Up a Tree

It's not just about food. Food, in fact, is really just a small part of it. Look around you at how we use domestic plants—as the fiber and color of our clothes, in the construction of our homes, for the paper of this book—I wouldn't be surprised if the ink with which it's printed came from soybeans. Wild plants can be used in the same ways—maybe even more. And those ways are worth knowing.

What camp is complete without a campfire, for example? Nothing is more comforting, even on a hot summer evening, than a campfire. (Have you ever noticed how much better whiskey is straight from a tin cup, staring into a campfire, with just a bit of a nip in the autumn air? Oh, man . . .) If you enjoy camping and do much of it at all, you would do well— very well, in fact—to know something about your firewood. Plains Indians preferred cottonwood for their tipi and earth lodge fires. It has a pleasant smell, it's easily gathered and broken up for a fire, "squaw wood" twigs snapped from a larger tree are a great fire starter, it burns hot and clean (although it's not long lasting), and, most importantly when you're sleeping close to a fire in a closed shelter, it doesn't throw sparks.

Ash splits easily, burns hot, and ignites even wet or green. For long-lasting coals, of course, you want a hard wood like oak or walnut; hickory if you can find it. Thirty years ago I was a bachelor, spending weekends in my ancient log house down in the Loup River bottoms here on my land in central Nebraska. The day I am thinking of, a blizzard was raging outside my cozy walls, my woodstove was glowing and smoking away, keeping everything toasty. I had a guest that day, Moose Osterman, the barber and champion fisherman up in town. We were enjoying hot chocolate laced with peppermint schnapps and listening to the wind howl outside.

"What kind of wood do you burn in that?" he asked, pointing at the stove.

"Uuuuh . . . tree wood," I said lamely. I knew there were

different kinds of trees but hadn't really given the qualities of their wood much thought.

"No, I mean, what *kind* of wood . . . cottonwood? Russian olive? Ash? Hackberry?"

"Well, Moose, to tell you the truth, I really hadn't given that much thought. I just gather whatever I can find down and dry, cut it up, haul it here to the cabin, and throw it into the ol' Bucks Hot Blast."

"You should get to know your woods, Roger. There's a lot of difference, and it's worth knowing about. Thing is, during the day when you don't mind carrying wood in and ashes out, that's the time to burn your cottonwood or Russian olive. When it gets really cold, maybe a little windy, start using your split ash or oak. When the temperature drops below freezing, the winds blowing, maybe there's a little snow in the air, you want that fire to keep going all night long so you don't have to get up and stoke the stove when all you really want is to be warm and cozy under the covers. So that's when you throw in a big hunk of unsplit oak or ash just before you go to bed. Be sure you close down your draft and dampner"—Moose said it that way: "dampner." "When it gets down around zero, the wind is howling, snow blowing in through the cracks of the house, come bedtime you want to stuck the biggest piece of unsplit wood you can find into that stove, close everything down, and maybe pack some magazines around the log so no air can get at it, and it'll perk away all night long, just enough to keep some warmth in the house so you don't have to crawl out of bed and come down that ladder from the loft to stoke the stove."

I was soaking all this valuable information up, as you can imagine, and Moose paused to let me appreciate the wisdom he was sharing, and to set me up for his final bit of advice: "But when the temperature is well below zero and you can hear the trees popping outside . . . when the wind is shaking the house and little piles of snow build up under the doors and around the windowsills . . . that's when you use the biggest piece of unsplit walnut or hickory you have, close everything on the stove down, pack it with magazines, and then, just before you go up the ladder to bed, drink three beers. That way you're going to have to get up anyway, and while you're up, you might just as well go ahead and throw another log onto that fire."

Genius. Pure genius.

Trees give us fruit and nuts—although sometimes it's not all that obvious: The humble hackberry is edible and really quite good when ripe. They are mostly pit, like a lot of wild fruits, but if you are tramping along a wooded trail and spot a hackberry, grab a quick handful of the dark, matured berries and pop them into your mouth. Eat them like sunflower seeds, spitting out the pits. I don't suppose there is a lot of nutrition there, but hey—it's free food!

And maybe more. There was a major street in a city where I once lived, lined for miles with hackberry trees. One fall when the timing was just right, the ripe hackberries fell to the ground into puddles of rainwater, where whatever sugars they had in them fermented. Robins—which love berries—gobbled them up . . . and got thoroughly sloshed in the process. Robins are generally viewed as cheerful birds (their manic squawking drives me nuts!), but the city quickly learned that robins are very bad drunks. They challenged perfectly civil pedestrians, passing dogs, even automobiles, blocking the sidewalks, picking fights, intimidating even large dogs. I have no idea what hackberry wine would taste like, but I can tell you for a fact that it acts on robins like Jack Daniels on a farm boy.

Trees also give us sap for syrup. It's a lot of work, but nothing beats homemade maple syrup. If you live in an area where there aren't many maples, look around for box elders. They're a member of the maple family, and many Indian tribes tapped them for their sweet sap.

Kinnikinnick or red willow, sometimes dogwood, provides the inner bark that provided smoking materials for all those Indian peace pipes. A few twigs from an apple tree will do wonders for an otherwise undistinguished pipe tobacco. I smoke my own homemade hams with apple wood and corncobs—the sweetest smoke you can imagine. You just want to sit in that smokehouse with the hams and bacon hanging from the rafters and breathe it in!

A Botanical Bounty

I sometimes wonder if there is actually such a thing as "useless vegetation" so reviled by the Lincoln City Weed Inspector oh! so many years ago. Everything seems to have found a use somewhere along the line at some time or another. Bedweed catchstraw earns both its names. All you have to do is walk through a patch or pass your arm through it and you will understand the part about "catchstraw." The stuff grabs you like half a dozen kids passing through the grocery store candy aisle. And it was the stuffing of choice for pioneer mattresses—thus "bedweed," for its flexibility and loft. Papyrus is another name for sedge, the tall reeds that grow common in wetlands; its fibers provided us a foundation for some of our first efforts at easy, portable, flexible written texts.

Scouring rush (also called horsetail, snake grass, pop grass, joint grass . . .) has a rough surface from the silica it pulls from the soil and concentrates in its skin; it was used by the Indians for sanding down arrow shafts, and by the pioneers to scour pots and pans. Pennyroyal was used by Plains Indians as a mosquito repellent, and can still serve the camper to that purpose when he can find it—it seems to be getting increasingly rare as the mosquitoes grow increasingly worse. Or maybe it's a matter of the mosquitoes growing increasingly worse as the pennyroyal gets increasingly rare.

Not to forget the beauty of flowers. Sure, some flowers are edible (violets and daylilies, for example), but some are poisonous and yet still breathtakingly beautiful . . . like my favorite, the iris. Beauty is enough as far as I am concerned. Our land is populated with naturally occurring gayfeather and spiderwort, which, their names aside, are stunningly beautiful flowers. This year we have had a wet and cool July, which is apparently precisely what morning primrose likes because our place and the land for miles in every direction is virtually paved with the brilliant pale yellow of primose. As far as I know there's nothing edible on primrose. There doesn't have to be. It is beautiful enough to my eye that it nourishes me nonetheless.

A Final Word on Published Resources Despite My Promise Not to Give You Any Such Thing

Despite the fact that I am not going to try to put together an extensive bibliography for you, I would like to suggest a couple of books that I have found useful. When I started my investigations into wild foods forty years ago, there was almost nothing. I scrambled for references and bought everything I could find on bookstore shelves. Now there is more than I can easily deal with in the limited space of an appendix, not to mention a sidebar. Believe me, if you go to your library or bookstore, you are going to find more than you can wade through or afford with comfort.

Euell Gibbons's wonderful series starting with *Stalking the Wild Asparagus* (originally published by David McKay Company, New York, in 1962 but still in print and available from a variety of publishers . . . just go to www.amazon.com and you'll have more choices than you can easily sort through in an hour) is still a classic because it is accurate, helpful, and, best of all, wonderful reading. (I am delighted to say that Euell Gibbons endorsed my run for the Lancaster County Weed Control Authority back in 1973. I still have his letter around here somewhere.) Bradford Angier wrote a series—dozens!—of *Free for the Eating Wild Foods* and wilderness survival books (Stackpole Books, Mechanicsburg, Pennsylvania) through the 1960s that are still favorites of mine, still available from amazon.com, new, used, battered, or mint. Other real classics include *Sturtevant's Edible Plants of the World* (edited by U. P. Hedrick, originally published in 1919 by J. B. Lyon, Albany, for the State of New York Department of Agriculture's 27th annual report, Vol. 2, part II) and republished in 1972 by Dover. This is primarily an index to wild foods but is full of very useful information beyond a simple listing.

I have always been fond of *Edible Wild Plants of Eastern North America* by Merritt Lyndon Fernald and Alfred Charles Kinsey, originally published in 1943 but revised by Reed C. Rollins and republished by Harper and Row in 1958. My copy is worn to a frazzle, and I suspect it won't be easy to find another one, unless I am ready to pay a premium price for a "collector's" copy. But this is a terrific resource of excellent information and, what's even better, I love the notion of one of the coauthors being Alfred Kinsey. Yes, that is *the* Alfred Kinsey of the Kinsey Sex Institute! He was into weeds before he was into sex, as it turns out. I don't want to make any promises here, but he may have been on to something. *All About Weeds* by Edwin Rollin Spencer is also a Dover reprint (1974, from the original published by Scribners in 1940 and 1957); it's another volume I keep on my quick-access shelf.

By far my favorite resource, which has been mentioned already many times in these pages, is Kay Young's *Wild Seasons: Gathering and Cooking Wild Plants of the Great Plains*

(University of Nebraska Press, 1993). There are a lot of side issues for me here—I know and love Kay, and I know she is a solid, careful researcher. I know she has cooked up all of the recipes she's offered, and I've even sampled some. She is an academically trained folklorist and therefore knows exactly where to look for traditional materials like wild food sources and information. And her book deals with precisely the region I know best, love most, and want to know the most about, the central Plains.

Believe me, it will be worth your while to spend a couple of hours shopping around for books you find most useful for your own interests, region, and reading and eating tastes. Don't take my word for it; drop by your nearest library or bookstore soon and do some bibliographic foraging before you head for the woods and pastures.

Index to Plants

About the Author

Roger Welsch is a well-known humorist, folklorist, and essayist. For years he hosted "Postcard from Nebraska," a biweekly feature on CBS's *Sunday Morning* with Charles Kuralt. He is the best-selling author of *Old Tractors and the Men Who Love Them*, *Diggin' In and Piggin' Out*, *My Life with Dogs*, and more than twenty-five other titles.

Welsch was adopted into the Omaha Tribe in 1967 and received official designation as tribal friend by the Pawnee in 1995. Welsch resides in Dannebrog, Nebraska, with his wife, Linda, and his dogs, Dunstan and Abigail.